THE DUKE
OF THE
ABRUZZI
An Explorer's Life

ghiacciaio E.

THE DUKE
OF THE
ABRUZZI
An Explorer's Life

MIRELLA TENDERINI & MICHAEL SHANDRICK

THE MOUNTAINEERS

BÂTON WICKS

Published by The Mountaineers
1001 SW Klickitat Way, Suite 201, Seattle, WA 98134

Published simultaneously in Great Britain by Bâton Wicks Publications, London.
All trade inquiries to: Cordee, 3a DeMontfort Street, Leicester, England, LE1 7HD

10 9 8 7
5 4 3 2 1

Manufactured in the United States of America

Edited by Mary Anne Stewart
Cover design by Patrick Lanfear
Book design by Alice C. Merrill
Book layout by Ani Rucki

Frontispiece: *On the Baltoro Glacier*

Library of Congress Cataloging-in-Publication Data
A catalog record for this book is available at the Library of Congress.
ISBN 0-89886-499-2 (North America)

British Library Cataloguing in Publication Data
A catalogue record for this book is available at the British Library.
ISBN 1-898573-18-2 (U.K.)

Table of Contents

𝒞

Foreword

Of the great adventure travelers, none has been so much in my thoughts as Luigi Amedeo di Savoia, the Duke of the Abruzzi. I can say that of the greatest explorers of the past, from whom I have always drawn inspiration for my goals, it is he, above all, whom I have carried in my mind during my travels in the most arduous and untouched areas of the world. On the Alps and on the Himalayas, in Alaska and in the polar regions, on the Mountains of the Moon and on K2, in particular, it is this noble hero with whom, within my limits, I have most identified. However, I have also felt a kinship with him in the sorrows of a life full of contradictions and deceptions, in which responsibility, dignity, integrity—and even the success that in spite of all can reward someone who has paid for it dearly—are stubbornly never forgiven.

This book recounts the exploits of one of the greatest explorers and conquerors of frozen ranges, polar expanses, and mysterious rivers. But above all from these pages emerges the portrait of a pure idealist, steadfast in his principles, determined in his actions, and inspired by the solemn greatness of nature: qualities deserving of approval and praise and that give the measure of the man he was. Too often, however, these values were denigrated by mediocre men who did not know how to recognize them, just as they still do not know how to measure themselves by them.

I express my appreciation to the authors of this book for having been able to render, with so much sensitivity and balance, the real historical profile of this magnificent gentleman of the most elevated qualities and the most noble-minded interests: the last of a special breed.

I have but one regret with regard to the Duke of the Abruzzi: to have not lived in his time. Who knows, perhaps I would have found myself in his group of guides, tied into his rope on K2.

Walter Bonatti

Preface and Acknowledgments

I
n his own time the exploits of Luigi di Savoia, the Duke of the Abruzzi, made him famous on several continents. Today, however, his name is little known outside the mountaineering community, where he is remembered for mastering the Abruzzi Spur on K2. His original reknown is understandable for the Duke was a fascinating figure: a mountain climber and explorer, a diplomatic envoy for his king, and commander in chief of the Allied fleet in the Adriatic during World War I, a crown prince of Italy who, for mysterious reasons, renounced the American woman he loved.

The historian's task in recreating his life is complicated by the fact that the Duke's personal diaries were apparently lost when the Savoy family archives were destroyed in the closing days of World War II and because, while he wrote literally hundreds of letters to a wide variety of correspondents, the vast majority of these are very formal and reveal little of the Duke's personality. Most earlier biographies, all published originally in Italian, focused for this reason mainly on his explorations, for which, in any case, first-hand documentation exists in the splendid volumes authored by the Duke and Filippo De Filippi.

Another challenge was to sort out the contradictory accounts of various events in the Duke's life; Italian newspapers and magazines often had a strikingly different view of the activities of their crown prince than did English or American newspapers. Finally, the myths that had grown up around this extraordinary man—a very public personage who by nature was an extremely private individual—had to be turned into fact.

This book would not have been possible without modern technology. One author lives in Vancouver, British Columbia, the other divides her time between the Italian Alps and the south of France. We have never met face-to-face but were able to communicate quickly and effectively by exchanging faxes, e-mail messages, and computer diskettes. Each of us wrote individual chapters on some aspect of the Duke's career; we then exchanged these base texts, resolved discrepancies, added material as necessary, made further refinements, and finally created finished manuscripts in both English and Italian. It was an exciting and challenging effort, and we hope we have succeeded in bringing to life Luigi di Savoia, the Duke of the Abruzzi.

Mirella Tenderini and Michael Shandrick

Acknowledgments (M. Tenderini)

I cannot mention all the libraries and archives I visited, but I wish to thank all those who assisted me in my search at the Archivi di Stato in Milan and Turin, at the Società Geografica Italiana in Rome, at the Istituto Geografico Militare in Florence, at the Ufficio Storico della Marina, at the Alpine Club and at the Royal Geographical Society in London, and especially the staff at Fondazione Sella in Biella, where I spent much time consulting the correspondence between Vittorio Sella and the Duke of the Abruzzi as well as Sella's diaries—an inestimable source of first-hand information. I am especially grateful to Lodovico Sella for his friendly help and also for granting us the right to reproduce photographs by his great uncle Vittorio. Most of the photos were provided by the Museo della Montagna "Duca degli Abruzzi" in Turin: I thank Emanuela De Rege for her research and the Director of the Museum, Aldo Audisio, for his never-ending help in supplying me with information and putting me in touch with individual sources and archives.

Some individuals were of particular assistance and their contributions were very important: Generale Giovanni Braca, the only surviving person who knew the Duke personally, who told me touching anecdotes, and Professor Ernesto Milanese, who generously made available to me the results of his research on the Duke's enterprise in Somalia and otherwise provided encouragement. I also owe my thanks to Isa Venturati, Carlo Graffigna, Roberto Mantovani, Enrico and Mari Ercolani, Aroldo Benini, Admiral Sicurezza, Miri Ercolani, President of Montagna Avventura 2000, and many others who I hope will forgive me for not mentioning them, although they can be assured of my gratitude. I wish to thank Donna DeShazo, publisher of The Mountaineers Books, for having faith in this book, and Cynthia Newman Bohn and Mary Anne Stewart for their intelligent supervision. I thank my husband, Luciano Tenderini, for expertly checking the mountaineering passages in the book. Finally, I wish to thank the Duke's grandnephew, Amedeo di Savoia-Aosta for the documents he gave me and, especially, for telling me family stories which were invaluable to my understanding of what kind of man was hidden behind the official image of the Duke of the Abruzzi.

Acknowledgments (M. Shandrick)

The task of completing my part of this history was made possible through the support of many individuals. The most important person, and my chief angel, is my wife Gayl who guided me to the decision to do the book and then belayed me on the long climb. I also owe deep thanks to Michael Larkin of Poole, Dorset, whose "hobby" provided me with a wealth of essential data from the U.K.

I would also like to thank Dr. Bill Petrosky, who generously lent me the Duke' s expedition books from his bookstore in Portland, Oregon, and to his son Jim, who brought them to me in Canada. Most hearty thanks to those who gave me their time and access to various resources, especially Lee Norton of San Diego for her most generous help with the Elkins family archives; Katherine Kelly Elkins of Elkins, West Virginia, for her stories and suggestions; Mariam Touba, reference librarian at the New York Historical Society, for her assistance in locating articles on the Duke's activities in America; climber David Jones of Vancouver for his timely offers of consulting work, which helped keep this project alive; and the staff of the West Point Grey branch of the Vancouver Public Library for their consistently cheerful assistance. I also express my appreciation to George Hamilton of the British Columbia Mountaineering Club Library, Audrey Salkeld, Jon Waterman, Dr. Henry Osmaston, Joy M. Tukahirwa of Makerere University, Uganda, and the staff of the Whyte Museum, Banff, Alberta, Canada.

Lastly, I would like to thank Donna DeShazo, whose idea it was to do this book with me as far back as 1984, and to acknowledge the invaluable assistance of Mary Anne Stewart in putting the text in final form for publication.

Prologue

It was burning hot that twenty-second day of February 1933 as the combined troops of the Italian Colonial Army stood at attention on the simmering wharf at Mogadishu in Italian Somaliland. Long columns of grim-jawed soldiers of the Italian Army, black-shirted men of the Italian Fascist militia, and African soldiers of the Somali reserves waited in the oppressive heat, ready to pay the sixty-year-old Duke of the Abruzzi his final honor.

Finally, a slim figure with short-cropped gray hair emerged on the deck of the ship that had brought him from Italy. Wearing a civilian summer suit, the Duke pressed heavily on his cane yet stood ramrod straight, as he always had.

Visibly weak and suffering, consumed by cancer, he descended from the ship to the wharf with great effort. Holding his body erect, he slowly reviewed the troops, stopping several times to look into the eyes of the young soldiers, his dry lips curved in a melancholy smile.

His face was worn, yet there was still a familiar glint in his blue eyes. One of the most famous explorers of his age, a prince of the ruling House of Savoy, and an admiral in the Italian navy, his entire life had been a testimony to his strength of heart and nobility of purpose. In every aspect of his remarkable achievements he had known not only how to bury physical pain but also his emotions, keeping disappointments and passions hidden under the cumbersome burdens of loyalty and duty. Grueling as the effort was to review the troops, this now frail man who had walked hundreds of miles of unexplored land in the Arctic, Alaska, the Himalaya, and Africa had yet to walk another quarter-mile in the blistering heat before his duty would be done. Luigi Amedeo di Savoia-Aosta, the Duke of the Abruzzi, would not betray himself in the last official act of his very public life.

His dear friend Vittorio Sella, companion of so many expeditions, had tried to dissuade him from leaving Italy and interrupting his medical treatment. But the Duke had simply replied, somewhat bitterly: "Preferisco che intorno alla mia tomba s'intreccino le fantasie delle donne somale, piuttosto che le ipocrisie degli uomini civilizzati." ("I prefer that around my tomb there be entwined the fantasies of Somali women, rather than the hypocrisies of civilized men.")

Luigi di Savoia spent his final days on the farm he had created thirteen years earlier as an agricultural experiment in Somaliland's landscape. Before his arrival, this arid land of red dust some 80 miles (129 kilometers) from Mogadishu had been swept clean of any vegetation by the desert winds. Now bountiful crops grew in irrigated fields for miles in every direction. Where once a few starving nomadic tribes roamed in search of food and fought each other savagely over meager watering holes now stood modern farm buildings and houses containing small cottage industries. Tribesmen now labored together and prospered from their work.

The Duke had lived to see his dream of a successful agricultural experiment take root in this harsh land, a land from whence it was said the biblical plagues of drought, famine, and locusts had been sent to Egypt in the time of Joseph. Luigi di Savoia had given up Italy for this desert land where he had seen something precious, a land where legend also says that the three Magi had come to gather the aromatic woods of frankincense and myrrh as gifts for the Christ child. Fittingly, Somaliland would become his final resting place.

The Duke spent his last days in a plain house he had built for himself in the village. An unpretentious man in most respects, he had furnished it sparsely to meet his simple needs. The only adornments were photographs of a stunning, dark-haired woman. Several such photographs stood on the dresser in the Duke's bedroom, while another hung in the main room, next to a photograph of the Duke's cousin King Vittorio Emanuele III.

A deeply religious Catholic, on March 16 the Duke sent for a Franciscan friar to give him Holy Communion and the Last Rites. Two days later, at 2:00 A.M. on Saturday, March 18, 1933, Luigi Amedeo di Savoia-Aosta was dead.

None of the Savoy family were present at the funeral, although King Vittorio Emanuele III sent several crowns of flowers to the small gravesite. The governor of the colony, Maurizio Rava, had come to pay his respects the day before the Duke died, and it was he who made the funeral arrangements. Luigi di Savoia was buried in his admiral's uniform, an honor guard of Italian sailors served as pallbearers.

The news of the Duke's death spread rapidly throughout the region, and during transport of the coffin, thousands of Somalis, not only from the Duke's Village but from all the neighboring villages as well, hastened to pay their respects to the man they considered a father and benefactor. They wept and sang funeral laments; many had cut their hair as a sign of mourning. In the middle of the procession, a military airplane sent by the Italian colonial authorities flew overhead, dropping flowers on the funeral cortege.

In Italy, the news of the Duke's death stirred a wave of sometimes self-serving national pride. The king declared an official court mourning for twenty days following the Duke's death. Pope Pius XI, himself an accomplished mountaineer who as a young priest had wished to accompany the Duke on his North Pole expedition, sent an official message of condolence. Prime Minister Benito Mussolini closed a speech in Parliament with inflated rhetoric: "Today, the half-masted pennants of the Black Shirts bow in front of the body of the Savoy Prince in an act of reverence and love. He leaves us to reach the Great Shades and we salute him with a call that echoes mightily from the shores of our Mother Land to those of the Indian Ocean."

From beyond the grave, the Duke might have smiled curtly at the outpouring of tributes. Even in death, he could not escape from what he most abhorred in life: the hypocrisies of civilized men.

Chapter One

℃

Birth of an Explorer

LUIGI AMEDEO GIUSEPPE MARIA FERDINANDO FRANCESCO DI SAVOIA-Aosta was born in Madrid, Spain, on January 29, 1873, into the tumultuous political intrigues of a Europe that had been brokering power through war and royal alliances for centuries. His father, Amedeo di Savoia-Aosta, was a member of Italy's royal House of Savoy and at the time of Luigi's birth was the ruling king of Spain.

How Amedeo in 1870 had become the king of Spain was a not untypical story of the political upheaval of the times. The previous resident of the Spanish throne, the Bourbon queen Isabella II, had been deposed in 1868 by a "Glorious Revolution" aimed at establishing a Spanish republic. Worried that a wave of republican sentiment would sweep across the Continent, the royal heads of Europe had exerted enormous pressure on the Council of Ministers of the provisional revolutionary government to find a way to restore the monarchy.

As a compromise, the council finally decided to select a foreign king who would act under the constraints of a constitutional charter that limited his sovereignty. The compromise meant that Spain would still have a king, but one who could not interfere with the interests of the Spanish people. Not many princes were interested in the Spanish throne under these circumstances. It finally fell to Amedeo to carry out the wishes of his father, King Vittorio Emanuele II of Italy. The hero of Italian unification (the

Risorgimento), Vittorio Emanuele had in 1861 brought together into a constitutional monarchy many of the disparate Italian city-states that had been at war with each other for half a century. To maintain his own throne, Vittorio Emanuele needed all the European allies he could find. Duty bound as a Savoy to honor the head of his family, who was both his father and the king, Amedeo had no recourse but to accept the Spanish throne.

In contrast to his father, who was a charismatic leader and a cunning diplomat, Amedeo was gentle and tentative, an unambitious man who had grown up thinking that his older brother, Umberto, would be the next king of Italy and who was quite happy with the idea that he would always be a minor career soldier in the military. Nor was Amedeo ambitious in love. As expected of him by his family, he had dutifully married Princess Maria Vittoria Dal Pozzo della Cisterna, a woman who belonged to the wealthy aristocracy of Turin. Amedeo would have been happy to remain in Turin with his family for the rest of his life. He was reluctant, and by nature ill suited, to enter the volatile world of politics—least of all to become king of a foreign country.

When Amedeo arrived with his wife and two infant sons in Madrid on January 2, 1871, to assume the throne, he faced opposition from every quarter. The common people disliked him because he was not of Spanish blood. The Republicans hated him because he was royalty, while the pro-Bourbons viewed him as a poor replacement for their beloved Queen Isabella II. Amedeo's dislike for the trappings of royalty—he forsook his royal uniform for a tailored suit and often strolled through the streets of Madrid protected by a lone officer rather than riding in his ornate carriage surrounded by a company of guards—further alienated him from the Spanish aristocracy. Amedeo's spontaneous walks proved to be particularly imprudent considering his unpopularity. In July 1871, and again in July 1872, assassination attempts were made on his life.

At the time of Luigi's birth in January 1873, Spain was a powder keg ready to explode. Armed political factions on both the Right and the Left wanted to topple Spain's experimental constitutional monarchy. Troops led by the Bourbon heir, Don Carlos, fought government troops to reestablish a Bourbon throne. Battles between republican and government troops broke out in the provinces of Catalonia, Aragona, Navarra, and Basque, soon cutting Madrid off from the rest of the country. Amedeo was about to lose not only his throne, but perhaps his life and the lives of his family as well.

Isolated and unpopular on every front after a two-year reign, on February 11, 1873, King Amedeo abdicated the Spanish throne. Fearful of more assassination attempts, the family secretly left Madrid by train bound for Lisbon to stay temporarily with Amedeo's sister Maria Pia di Savoia and her husband, King Luis I of Portugal. Young Prince Luigi was just fourteen days old.

Amedeo and his family soon returned to Turin, the home of the Savoy family. A gracious and ancient city, Turin lay on the Po River, some 61 miles (98 kilometers) from Mont Blanc and a similar distance from Courmayeur, a mountain town in the Italian province of Aosta on the French border. There Amedeo and his wife resumed their lives in the solitude of the Palazzo Cisterna.

The family's life underwent another drastic change, however, when Luigi was just three and a half years old. In November 1876, his mother became ill and died. Amedeo's subsequent grieving wrecked his health. The loss of the Spanish throne, the death of his wife, and the responsibility of raising his three young sons alone turned him from a handsome thirty-one-year-old into a prematurely old man. Luigi and his two older brothers were often left to fend for themselves in the gloomy palazzo.

To relieve himself of the burdens of parenting, Amedeo sent his sons, one by one, to live at military schools. Thus in 1879, at six and a half years of age, Luigi was enrolled as a ship's boy in the royal naval academy, the Corpo Reali Equipaggi, in Genoa.

There are no records as to whether Luigi enjoyed naval schooling, but he was very diligent and got good marks. In enrolling him, Amedeo had instructed the boy's tutors, "No privileges for my son," but it was inevitable that as a prince of the country's ruling family, Luigi would always be considered different from his classmates. He would have to prove himself over and over just to earn the privilege of being treated like an ordinary student, and he was always expected to be the best student and the best athlete, as his rank of prince demanded.

During vacations from naval school, young Luigi often visited the vast, pristine game preserves of the Gran Paradiso massif, a frequent destination of his grandfather King Vittorio Emanuele II, a keen hunter of ibex, a wild mountain goat. This rugged, mountainous region of northern Italy is tucked into the Italian Alps 31 miles (50 kilometers) from Monte Cervino (the Matterhorn).

Many members of the Savoy family were good mountain hikers, and virtually all of them were mountaineers at some point in their lives. From an early age, one of the keenest of the family's mountain explorers was the robust and beautiful Princess Margherita di Savoia, the daughter of Ferdinando, the Duke of Genoa, the brother of King Vittorio Emanuele II. As a girl, Margherita's affection was for her first cousin Amedeo, but in 1868, at age sixteen, she was given in marriage to Amedeo's twenty-four-year-old brother Umberto, the heir to the throne.

Umberto brought his two mistresses with him into the marriage, and their presence made it convenient for Margherita to be away climbing in the mountains as much as possible, even after she gave birth to a son in 1869. Margherita retained her affection for Amedeo and also befriended his wife, who on her deathbed in 1876 asked the twenty-five-year-old Margherita to look after her three young sons.

Margherita's own father had died of illness while away at war in the Crimea when she was four, and having experienced life without a parent, she took her role as Luigi's protector seriously. While it is not recorded that she took him with her on her climbs, she instilled in him her passion for mountaineering.

The first person known to have actually taken Luigi into the mountains was Francesco Denza, a Barnabite friar. Denza was a scholar, scientist, and founder of the meteorological observatory at Moncalieri, near Turin. Because of Denza's reputation as an educator, Amedeo entrusted his three sons to him during the summers, which they spent mostly hiking and climbing rather than in the classroom. The Barnabite used the outdoors to teach the boys meteorology, geography, and geology, but, more importantly, he introduced them to mountaineering.

Across Italy, educators like Denza were among the forefront of those who believed that mountaineering was an essential training ground for young men in their spiritual, as well as their educational, development. A leading proponent of this movement was Quintino Sella, the austere finance minister of King Vittorio Emanuele II. Sella was also a brilliant mining engineer, geologist, and professor, as well as an excellent mountaineer. Unlike many of his contemporaries, he disliked the prevailing Christian asceticism because he

felt it promoted neglect of the body. Instead, he believed that a devout prac-
tice of mountaineering would foster perseverance, foresight, and courage—
attitudes he felt were missing among the young men of the day.

When Sella founded the Italian Alpine Club (the Club Alpino Italiano,
or C.A.I.) in 1863, he gathered in its ranks the best mountaineers of the
time. Most of them were, like himself, men of science who found spiritual re-
juvenation by exploring and studying the natural sciences in the mountains
and valleys of the Alps.

The mountaineering movement produced a series of C.A.I. centers in
cities nearest the Alps. Men living in the villages at the feet of the highest
peaks began working as guides and porters in the service of more and more
climbers arriving from the cities. Some would later become guides for young
men like Luigi di Savoia.

Sella's mountaineering movement also produced an excellent climber
within his own family—his nephew Vittorio Sella would later become a dis-
tinguished climber and world-renowned photographer who would accompany Luigi on three of his expeditions.

In addition to his naval education, Luigi was also being taught to take
his place as a member of the ruling House of Savoy. He learned that it took
more than ships and men to win battles. Leadership was necessary for victory, and as a prince he was expected to take on the burdens of duty and
leadership, just as his father and grandfather before him. Soon, he was told,
it would be time for him to take his place, because Italy needed leaders.

The people of Italy had fought bravely for the country's unification.
During peace, however, they were losing their enthusiasm for self-government
in the face of hard decisions. The wars of independence had cost the country more than it could afford, and more taxes had to be levied to cover the
deficit. Men who had fought as volunteers took to the streets to protest
newly imposed laws that penalized the poorest.

In 1869, finance minister Quintino Sella fixed a tax on ground flour
(the *tassa sul macinato*), and the cost of bread rose so high that it was beyond
the reach of the entire working class. Thus began a wave of grim economic
events that would worsen under a succession of prime ministers, each driven
from office by boycotts, riots, and other demonstrations.

The Parliament was still elected by male citizens over twenty-five years of age who could read and write and were able to pay a tax of at least 40 lire per year. In a country of 30 million citizens, only 70 out of every 100 people could read, and only 1 out of 60 people could vote. Much of the citizenry was apathetic, feeling that the inequities of the new government were as bad as those of the preceding regimes.

Strikes broke out, and businesses failed all across the struggling nation. Millions of people had no source of income, and vast numbers of people were virtually starving. Such was Italy when the new king, Umberto I, brother of Amedeo and uncle of Luigi, assumed the throne in 1878 upon the death of his father, Vittorio Emanuele II. Luigi's beloved aunt Margherita was now Queen Margherita.

It was in this context that Luigi learned his lessons in naval school. Through vigorous self-discipline, he went about his studies with a determination and concentration that would serve him well in later years. His reserved nature in the heat of school exams and naval exercises was often misunderstood as aloofness. It seems, however, that he understood at an early age the military axiom: the hotter the battle, the cooler the passions.

In 1889, at age sixteen, Luigi was rewarded by an appointment to midshipman (*guardiamarina*). Although his rapid rise in rank may have been due to the fact that he was a member of the ruling family, this is unlikely. He had already spent ten years in the most demanding of the country's naval schools, and any effort to slip by would have cost him his career at an early age. As evidenced constantly in his later life, Luigi never indulged in easy success.

Upon his promotion in 1889, Luigi was assigned to the *Amerigo Vespucci*, a wood-hulled sailing ship, and set forth on the first of his many world voyages. It was on the *Vespucci* that Luigi received news of his father's death in 1890. Although he had never been close to his father, he was now truly alone.

With the death of Amedeo, his firstborn son, Emanuele Filiberto, became the Duke of Aosta. King Umberto I named Vittorio Emanuele, the second-born son, Count of Turin, while seventeen-year-old Luigi Amedeo was designated the Duke of the Abruzzi.[1] Luigi's one-year-old stepbrother, Umberto Maria, the child of his father's second marriage to Maria Letizia Bonaparte, was named the Count of Salemi.

The voyage of the *Vespucci* lasted almost a year and a half. After sailing to Greece, the ship left the Mediterranean and crossed the Atlantic to the southern tip of South America, where it passed through the Strait of Magellan into the Pacific and then made its way back to Italy.

During the *Vespucci's* long voyage, Luigi became friends with a young lieutenant named Umberto Cagni. Ten years the Duke's senior, Cagni was a born leader and a charismatic individual who became an important role model for the impressionable young man. An engaging, energetic personality, Cagni was also a very private person who could be stern if necessary. He had a penetrating gaze that quickly warmed to those who shared his interests and enthusiasms. Cagni would become the Duke's most faithful companion—taking part in many of his expeditions and serving him loyally throughout his naval career.

When the voyage of the *Vespucci* ended in 1891, the eighteen-year-old Duke received an appointment as second in command (*ufficiale in seconda*) of the torpedo boat 107S. In June 1893, he was appointed first lieutenant and in August was named second in command aboard the *Volturno*, a gunboat named after the site of a famous battle won by Garibaldi in 1860. That same month the crew was ordered to set sail for duty in the Indian Ocean off the coast of East Africa. Their mission was to quell an anticipated revolt in Italian Somaliland.

By 1885, most European countries had already established colonies all across Africa, taking advantage of the continent's vast mineral deposits and other resources to fuel the growth of European industry and expansion. Germany had occupied Togo, Cameroon, and Tanganyika. France had annexed Madagascar, while Belgium consolidated its possession of the vast rubber deposits in the Congo. Britain had occupied nearly the whole of the east coast of Africa, including a part of Somaliland.

In contrast, Italy had been slow to colonize Africa. Its first African possession, Eritrea—a small desert region between the Red Sea, Ethiopia (Abyssinia), the Sudan, and British Somaliland—was not acquired by exploration or conquest, but was purchased in 1882 from an Italian trader who himself had bought the bay of Assab and the surrounding land from the Eritreans. By 1885, Italy had signed agreements with four Muslim sultans granting the rights to more land in Abyssinia and Somaliland.

Italian Somaliland was not the pick of the spoils in Africa. The land was bleak and uniformly hot and was therefore considered valueless by every other European nation. Furthermore, the many nomadic tribes were fiercely independent and difficult to control. Not too surprisingly, Italy's efforts to establish a colony were met with severe opposition.

Early in 1893 hundreds of rioters stormed Italian businesses in Mogadishu and fought with the local militia in the cities of Kismayu and Merca. The gunboat *Staffetta* was sent to quell the rebellion. When it arrived in the wide harbor of Mogadishu, the vessel aimed its 4.7-inch guns at the crowd milling on shore and fired. Seconds later, hundreds of Somalis lay dead amid the smoke.

This severe demonstration of Italy's military power should have put a stop to any notion that it could be driven out of Somaliland. Yet beneath the surface, tensions between the Somali people and Italians were increasing, and by August it was clear that another revolt was imminent.

The *Volturno* arrived in Mogadishu in September, and as the light gray gunboat slowly positioned itself in the harbor, the Somalis watched and waited on the shore. Certain of the consequences if they revolted again, the people dispersed, and the demonstrations against the Italians ceased.

The *Volturno* remained in the harbor for a month, giving the Duke a chance to set foot on East African soil. As tensions died down, the excited young officer ventured inland and along the coast, seizing every opportunity to explore this exotic land. He had fallen in love with Somaliland at first sight.

Chapter Two

𝒞

Scrambles
amongst the Alps

THE YOUNG DUKE'S COMPACT FRAME WAS BECOMING STRONG THROUGH the rigorous naval discipline of voyages at sea. His body was hardened even further during his increasingly difficult climbs throughout the Alps, which he undertook during summer shore leaves between 1892 and 1894.

The monthly magazine of the Club Alpino Italiano, headquartered in Turin, reported that in 1892, Luigi di Savoia climbed Punta Levanna, a 11,031-foot (3,362-meter) peak on the French border in the western Alps. The route, considered strenuous but not technically difficult, was the nineteen-year-old Duke's first important summit. It is recorded that his companion on the climb was Francesco Gonella, a successful Turin attorney and president of the C.A.I. Gonella would partner Luigi di Savoia on many of his early alpine ascents and would also accompany him on his first major expedition.

Luigi di Savoia's success on Punta Levanna encouraged him to climb higher and more difficult peaks, and he soon climbed the 13,323-foot (4,061-meter) Gran Paradiso in Italy's Graian Alps, not far from his boyhood home in Turin.

Luigi then turned to the Mont Blanc massif. He climbed the classic routes and reached Mont Blanc's 15,771-foot (4,807-meter) summit, adding this peak to his growing list of conquests. Mont Blanc was followed by a climb of the Dent du Géant ("The Giant's Tooth"), a 13,169-foot (4,014 meter) peak, then considered quite a daring ascent.

As guides for his climbs the Duke relied on the so-called Valdostani, who took their name from a mountainous region north of Turin known as the Val d'Aosta, which included the villages of Courmayeur and Valtournanche. Like their counterparts in France and Switzerland, the Valdostani were originally chamois hunters or crystal seekers whose vast knowledge of the mountains made them expert guides. The Valdostani tended to specialize—those from Courmayeur concentrating on Mont Blanc and those from Valtournanche on the Matterhorn—but the best of the Val d'Aosta guides would no doubt have been at home on any mountain in the world.

Luigi climbed several routes on the spurs of Monte Rosa, a 15,203-foot (4,634-meter) massif near the Swiss-Italian border southeast of the Matterhorn, with the Valtournanche guide Antoine Maquignaz, who would later be part of the Duke's Mount Saint Elias expedition.

After Monte Rosa, Luigi and Maquignaz, along with two other guides, climbed the 14,690-foot (4,478-meter) Matterhorn—or Monte Cervino, as it is known in Italian—by the Breuil route.

By 1894, the Duke had completed a number of impressive alpine ascents, as recorded in an article written by Gonella for the Club Alpino Italiano magazine. These ascents included climbs and traverses of the 11,194-foot (3,412-meter) Aiguille du Moine, the 12,247-foot (3,733-meter) Petit Dru, the 11,302-foot (3,445-meter) Aiguille des Charmoz, and the 11,423-foot (3,482-meter) Aiguille du Grepon, all in the Mont Blanc range.

In the summer of 1894, the Duke arrived in Zermatt to climb Swiss peaks, accompanied by three Val d'Aosta guides—Emile Rey,[2] David Proment, and Laurent Croux—and his climbing companion Gonella. The group made several ascents, including climbs on the 14,293-foot (4,357-meter) Dent Blanche ("The White Tooth") and the 13,849-foot (4,221-meter) Zinalrothorn. It was quite natural that the party chose to climb these long, difficult routes, for they were preparing to attempt the Matterhorn from the Zmutt Ridge.

Edward Whymper, who in 1865 had been the first to reach the Matterhorn's summit, was fascinated by the snow-swept walls of the Zmutt Ridge—to him, nothing looked so completely inaccessible. The ridge had been successfully climbed only once—by the British climber Albert Frederick Mummery in 1879.

As it happened, Mummery and his favorite climbing partner, Dr. John Norman Collie, were also in the Alps during summer of 1894, their intent being to climb as many peaks as possible and to train for an upcoming attempt on Nanga Parbat, a Himalayan giant in the far western part of the British Punjab. One day, as the Duke and his companions were preparing for their ascent on the Zmutt Ridge, they ran into Mummery on the trails.

Sixteen years older than the Duke, Mummery listened with the ear of a mentor to the young prince's plans and then cautioned him against making the attempt because the Matterhorn was in poor condition that week. However, impressed by Luigi di Savoia's earnest commitment to climbing the route, Mummery invited the prince to join him on his next ascent.

Following their encounter with Mummery, the Duke and his guides left Zermatt and spent the rest of their time traversing the Dufourspitze and climbing the 14,940-foot (4,554-meter) Punta Gnifetti of Monte Rosa (which Queen Margherita had climbed the year before at age forty-two).[3]

The Duke had no sooner returned to Turin than he received a telegram from Mummery, who reported that the conditions on the Zmutt Ridge were now favorable and requested that the Duke proceed to Switzerland in all haste. The Duke quickly packed his bags and a few days later was again in Zermatt, to climb a route that had defied many fine mountaineers before and after Mummery. The Zmutt Ridge would certainly be the most difficult ascent the Duke had yet attempted.

At the time of Mummery's first ascent of the Zmutt Ridge in 1879, several futile attempts had been made on the route. Mummery, who climbed more by optimism and enthusiasm than by caution, had decided to work his way along a snow ridge 1,000 feet (305 meters) below the summit that was seemingly barred by a perpendicular section dropping straight to the bottom of the glacier. According to Mummery's account of the ascent in his book My Climbs in the Alps and Caucasus, he felt they would have to climb most of the way to the summit to see if a route, in fact, existed past this barrier.

On September 3, 1879, Mummery and his guides began climbing the route despite darkening skies and hurricane-force winds that forced a rival party to descend and abandon its attempt. After a sleepless overnight bivouac in the storm partway up the ridge, the four men made a brisk traverse of the final barrier to stand on top of the Matterhorn in the morning sun, having won the first ascent of the Zmutt Ridge.

A brief description of Mummery's second ascent with the Duke is also included in *My Climbs*. Early on the morning of August 27, 1894, Mummery led off across the broken boulders on the glacier followed by the Duke, Dr. Norman Collie, and their guide. From the base of the climb, Mummery chose to keep to the right of the track he had pioneered on the first ascent. They skirted the Tiefenmatten Glacier, turned straight up the mountain, and climbed until they reached a snow ridge.

Keeping an eye on an approaching storm, Mummery hurried their pace. In contrast to the conditions on Mummery's first ascent, the mountain this time was completely free of ice and snow. Mummery and Collie quickly led the last pitches without difficulty, and by 10:00 A.M., the Duke stood on the summit of the Matterhorn.

Enraptured by the climb and the camaraderie shared with his new companions, the twenty-one-year-old Luigi di Savoia pledged then and there to devote all his spare time and energy to mountain exploration. The vow could easily have been forgotten once the joy of the moment had subsided, but climbing was truly to become his life's passion.

Delighted that a royal prince had earned a summit on his own ability, the Turin division of the C.A.I. immediately honored the Duke's achievements by making him its honorary president. In addition, Mummery's influence in alpine circles resulted in the Duke's admission into the prestigious Alpine Club in London later that year.

The most important aspect of the ascent, however, was the long-lasting impression Mummery made on the Duke, despite, or perhaps because of, their completely different natures.

As a Savoy prince the first thing Luigi di Savoia learned as a small boy was not to display his emotions—a lesson that was further emphasized by his military training. In contrast, Mummery was outspoken in his views on climbing and was often found in the center of a debate, delivering his opinions with the biting wit for which he was known.[4]

The Duke, methodical and attentive to detail, possessed a naturally inquisitive and scientific mind and was relentless in his quest for scientific data, as he would demonstrate on all of his expeditions. Mummery, on the other hand, wrote in the preface of his book that he feared no contributions to science, topography, or learning of any sort would be found in it. He openly admonished those who looked for scientific evidence while climbing, often telling people he climbed solely for the fun of it. "To tell the truth," he wrote, "I have only the vaguest ideas about theodolites, and as for plane tables, their very name is an abomination."

The Duke's meticulous planning, which he pursued down to the most minute detail, was the hallmark of his expeditions. He would spend hours sorting and recounting items to make sure nothing was left undone. Mummery was often the victim of his overly optimistic personality. His lack of foresight caused him problems in provisioning throughout his climbing career. He also frequently failed to bring the right equipment or underestimated the difficulties of a climb or the weather.

Another difference was that Mummery was a commoner and had no royal expectations to live up to. He let his climbing define his status in the world. Luigi di Savoia, however, could not escape who he was in the eyes of the world. For him, climbing was a way of avoiding the public scrutiny that accompanied his position as a member of the ruling family of Italy.

The Duke no doubt appreciated the fact that Mummery treated him as simply another climber and not as royalty. As his later career would prove, the Duke wished to interact with people on equal terms rather than as prince and subject. He was unpretentious in manner, often preferring the company of his guides, simple, often illiterate, mountain peasants whom he viewed more as companions than as employees. Like Mummery, who wrote of the "pleasures of talk and contemplation" that he found with his companions in the mountains, the Duke valued the sense of brotherhood that arose from shared endeavors.

Finally, Mummery undoubtedly recognized a bit of himself in the Duke, whose competitive drive was evident even at this early point in his career. Mummery's unrelenting desire to seek new routes and conquer previously unclimbed peaks as well as his bold and aggressive style were to have a lasting impact on his royal colleague. The Duke's attraction to Mummery is perhaps the first appearance of what would become his infallible instinct for excellence and thus his ability to choose the most capable and compatible individuals for his expeditions.

On October 16, 1894, less than two months after his ascent of the Zmutt Ridge, the Duke set forth on another world circumnavigation with the Italian navy, a twenty-six-month voyage as a first lieutenant aboard the royal naval battle cruiser *Cristoforo Colombo*.

In December 1895, the *Cristoforo Colombo* stopped in Calcutta. During the ship's month-long stay, the Duke traveled across India with his close friend from the days of the *Vespucci*, 2nd Lieutenant Umberto Cagni, and 6th Lieutenant Filippo De Filippi, a young physician who would later achieve fame as the chronicler of the Duke's expeditions. The three visited Delhi, Agra, Benares, and Lahore. Near Darjeeling, they climbed a hill from which they could see 28,146-foot (8,579-meter) Kangchenjunga, the third highest mountain in the world. The Duke viewed his first Himalayan mountain thinking of his friend Mummery, now climbing Nanga Parbat somewhere amid so many other snow-capped peaks on the far horizon.

It was not until sometime during the *Cristoforo Colombo's* return voyage in 1896 that the Duke learned that Mummery and two Gurkha porters had perished on Nanga Parbat in August of 1895.[5] With the news of Mummery's death, the Duke began planning an expedition to 26,660-foot (8,126-meter) Nanga Parbat to avenge his friend, whose words still rang in his ears: "A true alpinist is the man who attempts new ascents."

The *Cristoforo Colombo* continued its voyage from Asia to Hawaii and then to the Canadian province of British Columbia. When he arrived on Vancouver Island at Victoria, the provincial capital of British Columbia, the Duke learned that a fifth expedition had just failed in their attempt to climb 18,008-foot (5,489-meter) Mount Saint Elias, located near the Alaskan coast on the border between Alaska and the Canadian Yukon.

Intrigued by the notion of climbing a difficult Alaskan mountain, the Duke discussed the idea with Charles E. Fay, a Tufts University professor from Boston who was one of the founders of the Appalachian Mountain Club. Fay was relentless in his promotion of North American climbing and enthusiastically encouraged the Duke to attempt Mount Saint Elias. The Duke thought carefully about it but, still committed to his pledge to avenge Mummery on Nanga Parbat, postponed his plans for Alaska until another time.

By the time the *Cristoforo Colombo* sailed back into Venice harbor in December 1896, the Duke had virtually organized his own Nanga Parbat expedition. However, soon after his return to Italy, he was forced to abandon his plans. A deadly plague had spread across western India, and a famine was killing hundreds of people in the Punjab. The Indian government had closed all access to Nanga Parbat and to all other Himalayan mountains as well.

Still determined to mount an expedition in 1896, the Duke shifted his sights to Mount Saint Elias. Higher than the Duke had yet climbed and still unconquered, it would be a most worthy objective.

To prepare for the Mount Saint Elias expedition, the Duke did some climbing in the Alps during the summer of 1896. In August, he arrived in Courmayeur to climb the Southwest Face of the Grandes Jorasses, a chain of five summits all higher than 4,000 meters. As guides, he secured Laurent Croux, who had climbed with him before in the Swiss Alps, and Joseph Petigax, another Val d'Aosta guide with whom the Duke was to share many future adventures.

The day before the climb, the Duke asked Petigax and Croux to explore the face in hopes of finding a route to the summit. That evening, the two guides returned just before nightfall to the Hotel Royal, where the Duke and his Italian Alpine Club friend Francesco Gonella, who had come to watch the climb, were waiting for them.

Petigax, a taciturn man who was uncomfortable with lengthy conversation, simply told the Duke that the climb was feasible, but not advisable. He said they had arrived near the top without any particular difficulty but were forced down because of dangerous stonefall.

Gonella responded to Petigax in jest, suggesting that the stonefalls were an excuse to avoid the dangerous ascent and that the guides had not gone as high as they said they had.

Unperturbed, Petigax responded, "The stones do fall. Nonetheless, the summit will be yours tomorrow."

The next day, Petigax and Croux, along with another guide, César Ollier, led the Duke on the climb. According to later accounts of the ascent, at one point Petigax stopped and put his hand into a hole in the rock face. He then took out a piece of dried bread that he had left there the day before, quietly demonstrating that he had in fact reached this point earlier.[6] His guide's honor proved, he then turned and led the Duke to the summit of one of the pinnacles, which the Duke named Punta Margherita (13,336 feet; 4,065 meters), after his beloved aunt and queen.

The Duke was impressed by the unflappable Petigax, and the friendship begun between the two men that summer was to last many years. The Duke invited Petigax to serve as his chief guide on the planned Mount Saint Elias climb, a position Petigax was also to hold on the Duke's subsequent North Pole, Ruwenzori, and K2 expeditions.

A few years later (1898), through colleagues in the Alpine Club, Luigi di Savoia had learned that a team of English alpinists were studying a spire in the Aiguille Verte group near the Mer de Glace in the Mont Blanc range. He immediately sent a telegram to Petigax, asking him to go to the other side of Mont Blanc and see if the spire was, in his opinion, climbable. Petigax surveyed the route and wired back a single word: *"Venez"* ("Come"). The Duke and Petigax arrived a day before the English team and claimed the summit, which Luigi proudly named Aiguille Petigax, *aiguille* indicating a needle-sharp peak.

The excitement the Duke felt in organizing his first large-scale expedition was subdued by the conditions he found when he returned to Turin after his summer's climbs. The Italian economy was wrecked, and the government was in a shambles. It would appear self-indulgent for a member of the royal family to mount such an expedition during these troubling times, so he kept his plans secret.

Italy's problems centered around Abyssinia (Ethiopia), Italy's newest colony in Africa. War had broken out between Italian and Abyssinian forces in 1895, and after two early defeats, the Italian government had sent an army of ten thousand troops to conquer Abyssinia once and for all. However, on March 1, 1896, Italian forces underwent a stunning defeat at Adwa, where they fought against the warriors of the Abyssinian emperor, Menelik. Some five thousand Italian troops and two thousand native auxiliary troops had been killed or captured, and the colony had been lost.

At a time when Italy declared itself ready to sit at the same table as the major European powers, Adwa became an uncomfortable topic. The Italian army had suffered the worst colonial disaster of any European nation. More Italian lives had been lost in this single battle than in all the wars of Italy's independence put together, and the shame was felt throughout Italy.

Italy had many other problems to face beside the defeat in Abyssinia. Massive crop failures created hunger riots by people starving in the cities. Bank scandals caused revolts among unhappy depositors.

In the midst of these conditions, when the Duke mentioned to Queen

Margherita his plan to mount an expedition to climb Mount Saint Elias, the queen seized upon her nephew's idea as an opportunity to change prevailing public sentiment from despair to excitement and pride. King Umberto, who had previously demonstrated only lukewarm interest in his nephew's mountaineering, listened to the persuasive queen as she proposed that the monarchy support the Duke's expedition. Few other alternatives were available to enhance the image of the royal family, so Umberto finally agreed to sponsor the Duke's first real expedition.

Chapter Three

ℰ

Mount
Saint Elias

IT WAS A WARM DAY ON MAY 17, 1897, AT TURIN'S PORTA NUOVA RAILWAY
station as a hundred citizens gathered for ceremonies bidding the Duke and
his party of mountain climbers farewell on their expedition to conquer
Mount Saint Elias.

Escorted to the station by his second eldest brother, Vittorio Emanuele,
the twenty-four-year old Duke sported a thin mustache that made him look
somewhat more mature. He was dressed, as always, in a stylish traveling suit
and appeared self-assured, yet stern. Years of attending public events had
trained him to appear calm despite the fact he was about to represent all of
Italy on an expedition where he would carry not only his honor, but that of
his country, to the summit.

Traveling with him and serving as his aide-de-camp was his good friend
from the navy, Umberto Cagni. Francesco Gonella, the Duke's rope partner
on his early climbs in the Alps was also part of the group, as was Filippo De
Filippi, the lieutenant from the *Cristoforo Colombo* who had accompanied
the Duke in his travels around India in 1895 and who would serve as expedition doctor and diarist.

As expedition photographer the Duke had engaged Vittorio Sella, De
Filippi's cousin and the nephew of Quintino Sella, founder of the Italian
Alpine Club. Vittorio, then almost thirty-eight, had already gained an inter-
national reputation for the impressive photographs he had taken on three

expeditions to the Russian Caucasus. His work was acclaimed among art dealers in Britain, where he had sold 130 prints to the Royal Geographical Society in 1890. His fame had also been secured in Italy when he photographed Queen Margherita's climb of Punta Gnifetti to inaugurate Monte Rosa's summit hut in 1893.

Sella's mountaineering photographs were also widely known in the United States, thanks to Charles Fay, the Boston professor whom the Duke had consulted when he first became interested in Mount Saint Elias. Fay, who had become friends with Sella while climbing in Italy, arranged large exhibitions of Sella's prints up and down the East Coast. More than 20,000 visitors had come to see Sella's images at elegant galleries, as well as at the National Geographic Society.

In spite of his growing reputation, Sella, also a noted mountaineer, was nervous when the Duke invited him to photograph the Mount Saint Elias climb, feeling he could not live up to the Duke's expectations. "I am tortured by insomnia, and this elegant princely life, with the conviction that I will never be able to reward with my works the demonstration of kindness of the Duke," Sella wrote to his wife. "Instead of exciting me, the prospect humbles me." To help him on the Mount Saint Elias climb, Sella brought his assistant, Erminio Botta, who had accompanied him on two previous expeditions in the Caucasus.

The expedition would also include four guides (who had been sent on ahead to Liverpool, the port of embarkation). The Duke had designated Joseph Petigax, with whom he had climbed in the Alps the preceding summer, as chief guide. Petigax would be assisted by three old-school Val d'Aosta guides who had led the Duke and Gonella on earlier climbs in the Alps: Laurent Croux, Antoine Maquignaz, and Andrea Pellissier.

It was a surprise to some climbing purists that the Duke would bring Italian guides with him. However, previous climbers on Mount Saint Elias had said that if it was to be ascended at all, it would only be by experienced alpinists. The Duke had selected professional, expert mountain guides with records of long service in the Alps. He was aware that although the terrain was different, the glaciers of Alaska would require essentially the same climbing techniques used by his guides on the glaciers of the Alps. Most importantly, he knew that not a single important expedition in the world had succeeded without guides, including the previous attempts on Mount Saint Elias.

1 Father Francesco Denza, Luigi Amedeo (Duke of the Abruzzi), his brothers, Vittorio Emanuele and Emanuele Filiberto, and an unidentified figure

2 A rare clear day on the Agassiz Glacier during the expedition to Mount Saint Elias

4 *Mount Saint Elias from the Newton Glacier*

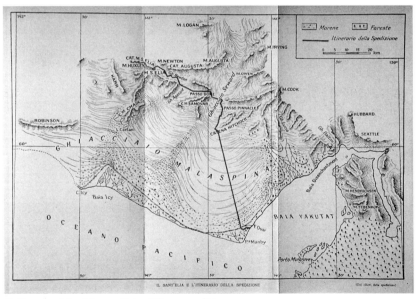

5 *Route of the Mount Saint Elias expedition*

◄ 3 *Icefalls on the Newton Glacier on the approach to Mount Saint Elias*

6 *Luigi Amedeo di Savoia-Aosta at age twenty-four, just after returning from Mount Saint Elias*

7 The Polar Star
caught in the ice
at Teplitz Bay

8 *Members of the North Pole expedition. In front (from left):*
Dr. Cavalli Molinelli, Evensen, Cagni, and Querini; in back,
Torgrisen, Andresen, and Stökken

9 Teplitz Bay from the east

10 Cagni's team after their return from achieving a farthest north record,
June 23, 1900. From left: Petigax, Fenoillet, Cagni, and Canepa

11 *Félix Ollier returns from hunting with a polar bear. Ollier, Stökken, and Querini disappeared during the attempt on the Pole and were never found.*

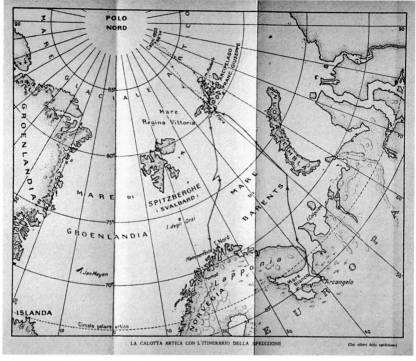

LA CALOTTA ARTICA CON L'ITINERARIO DELLA SPEDIZIONE   (Dai rilievi della spedizione)

12 Route of the Duke's polar expedition

So important were guides to this expedition—and so little had they been appreciated by many other alpine expeditions—that the Duke had founded a permanent institution to benefit the families of guides killed in the performance of their duties.

Mount Saint Elias was first discovered by European voyagers to the New World on July 20, 1741, when it was sighted by Vitus Bering from 120 miles (193 kilometers) out at sea. Although Bering did not name the mountain itself, he named a nearby point of land Cape Saint Elias, after the saint's day on which he spotted the peak. The region was next visited in 1778 by English explorer Captain James Cook, who inspected the mountain and named it after the cape.

Over the next century, explorers and mapping expeditions viewed the mountain and made calculations on the height of its summit but did not attempt a climb. In 1791, Italian explorer Alessandro Malaspina discovered a glacier estimated to be more than 80 miles (129 kilometers) long and more than 40 miles (64 kilometers) across at its widest, a distance greater than the state of Delaware. Eighty-three years later, in 1874, a mapping expedition from the U.S. Hydrographic Office officially named the massive sheet of ice and rock the Malaspina Glacier.

The Mount Saint Elias massif itself is a relatively easy climb technically. The difficulty lies in getting to the base of the peak and in dealing with the region's unpredictable weather. Five previous attempts on the mountain had failed because of the obstacles encountered on the march in.

To reach the base of the mountain, a party must travel across wide and difficult glaciers, carrying heavy loads of equipment and food. Rain, sleet, snow, or fog inevitably add to the problem of route finding. Lastly, climbers must negotiate a harrowing gauntlet of crevasses and collapsing ice seracs as they near the base of the mountain, where avalanches pour down on both sides of the route day and night.

Because the summit of Mount Saint Elias is more than 60 miles (97 kilometers) from the nearest forest vegetation, climbers are committed to the glaciers and are virtually isolated from any base of food supplies for a minimum of two months. Any minor repair, blunder, or lack of equipment could doom an expedition, as it had with the previous parties attempting to reach the summit.

The first large-scale climbing expedition to Mount Saint Elias took place in 1886, financed by the *New York Times*. Led by Americans Lieutenant F. Schwatka and W. Libbey and an Englishman, Lieutenant H. V. Seton-Karr, the party successfully landed near the mouth of the Yahtse River due south of the mountain and proceeded north into the lower range. Schwatka eventually reached 5,800 feet (1,768 meters) and Seton-Karr 7,200 feet (2,195 meters) before they were forced to turn back because their supplies were exhausted.

In 1888, two British brothers, W. H. Topham and E. Topham, and two Americans, G. Broke and W. William, followed Schwatka's route inland, reaching the flanks of the mountain at 11,483 feet (3,500 meters), but they too were forced to return because of inadequate supplies.

A scientific expedition sponsored by the National Geographic Society and the United States Geological Survey brought University of Michigan professor Israel C. Russell and topographer M. B. Kerr to Mount Saint Elias in 1890. Landing at the northwest corner of Yakutat Bay, the party crossed the tributary glaciers of the Malaspina and spent the next thirty days crossing the main glaciers until they reached Blossom Island, an oasis of vegetation on a frontal moraine. The party eventually made its way up the flanks of the mountain until a logistical mishap forced Russell to endure six days of storm alone in a tent without fuel and food. Too weak to continue, Russell was forced to abandon the climb.

Wiser for his efforts, Russell returned in 1891. However, as his expedition was unloading supplies in Yakutat Bay, a storm hit, capsizing two whaleboats carrying loads and drowning two men. Shaken by the losses, Russell's party continued on with the expedition, crossing the Malaspina Glacier to the treacherous Newton Glacier by a more direct route that took them to a col just below the ridge leading to the summit. Unfortunately the climbers arrived too late in the day to make an attempt on the summit— exhausted, low on supplies, and about to face yet another storm that could last for days, Russell reluctantly gave the order to turn back once again.

Russell's 1891 expedition was the last to attempt the peak prior to the Duke's attempt in 1897. Aware of problems previous parties had encountered in crossing the glaciers, the Duke decided to plan his expedition as if he were going to the North Pole instead of climbing a mountain.

Five days after leaving Turin, the Duke's party set sail for New York from Liverpool aboard the *Lucania*. The guides became seasick and spent the voyage in the second-class smoking lounge of the ocean liner, playing endless games of cards. On deck, the Duke and Sella busied themselves photographing the voyage and looking after the sixty cases of luggage, some containing new photographic equipment for the trip.

Almost from the start, the Duke was worried the Italians would not be the first to climb Mount Saint Elias. Just a few days before the expedition was about to leave, he had been informed by Professor Fay that an American party led by Henry S. Bryant of Philadelphia was already attempting the mountain. Arriving in New York City on May 28, 1897, the Duke's party was greeted by Professor Fay, who had brought along a small group of reporters. Surprised by the reception and not wanting to tip his hand, the Duke concealed his true mission, saying, "I am simply taking this trip for pleasure. I shall not remain in New York more than one night."

The party then took the train to San Francisco, where, housed in a hotel, they began to pack the large stock of food and equipment acquired for them by Professor Fay. The Duke joined in as the men worked late into the night for three days in a row, packing tinned meats and vegetables, condensed milk, preserved soups, navy biscuits, pasta, cheese, chocolate tablets, tea, dried fruits, salt, pepper, rum, olive oil, and mustard into fifty sacks and fifty sealed tins. By midnight on June 8, the Duke and his weary men weighed in their total food supply at 6,600 pounds—enough for ten men for fifty days.

While in San Francisco, the Duke met with M. B. Kerr, who had acted as topographer on the first Russell expedition. Together, they carefully went over the route from a map Kerr created for the Duke. The Alaska Commercial Company in San Francisco arranged to have one of its Alaska-based steamers alter its course and take the expedition from Sitka to Yakutat, the party's proposed landing site.

As he was planning the expedition, the Duke had also written to Russell himself, asking his advice about hiring porters. Feeling that the independent character of Americans might cause friction in an expedition headed by a royal prince, Russell suggested Major E. S. Ingraham, a Seattle outfitter, as a contractor who could keep things under control. Ingraham agreed to hire a team of ten porters for a period of three months, and he himself would accompany them on the expedition.

When the expedition arrived in Seattle the Duke met with the capable

Ingraham and his ten American porters, a mixed team of students, sailors, and common laborers, each of whom had been carefully interviewed by Ingraham and had passed a rigorous physical exam to qualify. On the Duke's behalf, Ingraham had also chartered a Seattle yacht, the *Aggie*, to transport himself and the porters to Sitka and Yakutat Bay.

In Sella's mind, the Duke was spending too much money. In Seattle, Sella picked up twenty packframes (one for each member of the party except the Duke), sledges, and double-layer leather boots that the Duke had had custom-made for the expedition. The rental of the *Aggie* had cost $2,000, and it would cost another $270 for the *Aggie* to be towed by a larger vessel into the dangerous entrance of Yakutat Bay. Each American porter was to be paid $35 per month, and Major Ingraham would receive $100 per month. In addition, hundreds of dollars had been paid for food, lodging, and transportation to and from America.

"The prince spends a lot and I would like to keep him from that or advise him not to squander so much money but I cannot," wrote a frustrated Sella in a letter to his wife.

While Sella worried about money, most of the men in Seattle had their minds set on making their fortunes. Gold had been discovered the summer before in the Yukon Territory of Canada, and thousands of gold-hungry miners thronged the streets of Seattle, trying to find passage north to the gold fields, where more than $600 million in ore was waiting to be found.

From Seattle, the Duke and his men sailed north through British Columbia's Inside Passage on board the *City of Topeka*, an old and slow 1,500-ton steamer. The journey left the men plenty of time to feast their eyes on the ever-increasing beauty of the blue waters and summer sunsets.

On June 20, the *City of Topeka* entered Sitka harbor, where the *Aggie* lay waiting for them with an Italian flag hoisted in welcome. The expedition's supplies were transferred from the *Topeka* to the Alaska Commercial Company's *Bertha*, an old port steamer that was to tow the *Aggie* into the dangerous entrance of Yakutat Bay, where a storm had sunk two boats from the second Russell expedition six years before.

On their arrival at Yakutat Bay, the Italians found it enshrouded in fog, but with calm waters. As the *Bertha* and the *Aggie* dropped anchor, scores of Indians from the village of Yakutat ran along the beach, waving a welcome with lighted pine torches. From an Indian guide, the Duke learned that

Bryant's expedition had landed nearby ten days before and was already on the move. There was little time to waste.

The Duke was aware that previous expeditions had cached their supplies on the beach and relied on wood found between the beach and the glacier for fuel, but he believed that the repeated trips required to carry wood and water over the moraine to reach the forward camps had weakened those parties and contributed significantly to their failure. The Duke had decided to avoid this situation by bringing oil cookstoves and by going directly to the glacier to set up camp.

The porters used small rowboats to transfer supplies from the *Aggie* to the beach, then the old steamer left for Sitka, an agreement having been made that the ship would return to Yakutat Bay on August 10. Even with the help of additional Indian porters, it took six days to transport the gear, luggage, and food from the beach to the glacier. Sorting through expedition stores and carrying loads from the beach through the woods were made more difficult by the swarms of hungry mosquitoes that were impervious to the insecticidal ointments the Italians had brought. The Duke's face was puffed by the many bites he received in the night, and the otherwise jovial men were agitated by a lack of sleep and the irritating insects.

By June 29, forty-three days after leaving Turin, the expedition was finally encamped on the snowy landscape of the Malaspina Glacier. There they loaded the four wooden sledges with some 3,000 pounds of supplies and watched them sink deep into the snow, where they stuck.

Sella's substantial photographic baggage alone weighed 235 pounds and included a large camera with attachments, two smaller cameras, a Ross and a Kodak, along with film canisters and accessories, a developing tent, and scores of photosensitive plates.[7] The expedition's small Mummery tents weighed only 3.5 pounds each, but the ten iron bedsteads the Duke had brought along might as well have been lead anchors.

Mummery had called such mountaineering beds a menace because they created a draft of cold air underneath the sleeper. Their worst fault, he said, was that the men who slept on them would be ridiculed in other parts of the world. "Out west, for some mysterious reason," Mummery chided, "it is considered unmanly to sleep otherwise than on the ground."

The Duke and four of his Italian colleagues slept on the foot-high beds. Ingraham and his ten porters, however, kept their opinions about their employer's sleeping apparatus to themselves and slept on the ground. Sella's assistant Botta and the Italian guides put their sleeping bags on the ground covered by mackintosh groundsheets and woolen blankets.

The sledge situation was finally remedied by modifying the runners, repacking the sledges, and adding ropes so that two men could pull while two others pushed, and on July 1, as the Alaskan sky was beginning to clear, the Duke gave the signal to march. He aimed the four sledges toward a point some 21 miles (34 kilometers) away, toward the junction of the Malaspina Glacier with the Hitchcock chain. Ahead of them across the glacier's wide expanse lay nothing but a thick mantle of snow.

Despite the added muscle of Ingraham's Americans, the men could only push the sledges for twenty minutes at a time before needing to rest. As the fog descended upon the party, the Duke used some of his navigation experience to help guide them. Tying himself some distance behind the lead sledge on a taut rope, he used a compass to guide the sledge, and the others followed. With the fog becoming thicker, it took five hours to cover 6 miles (10 kilometers) on the first day.

For the next two days, the march was repeated in much the same manner. The men pushed, grunted, and sweated in the pale, diffused light. The oil cookstoves were fastened firmly to the sledges, allowing the party to cook as they traveled. Sometimes fog mixed with the bright reflection of the snow. Whatever time of day, the ever-present mist, fog, rain, and snow concealed any landmark.

Throughout this ordeal, the Duke displayed exceptional physical stamina. Frustrated at the slow progress, he pushed ahead to scout out a location for the next camp. He returned after some five hours and did not even appear to be tired, although he had been carrying a fifty-pound pack.

Finally, on July 3, the mist lifted just enough for the Italians to spot a dark line of detritus at the base of the Hitchcock chain. Soaked in sweat and exhausted after covering the last 8 miles (13 kilometers) in one day, the men were delighted to see anything other than the unremitting white of snow and ice. The passage of the Malaspina Glacier had been accomplished.

The Italians set up camp on the glacier, while the Americans pitched their tents in a small grassy valley just beyond it. The next morning, Ingraham visited the Duke to receive the day's instructions. The Duke greeted him and said, "I see this is your Independence Day. You may make it a holiday." The Americans held a flag-raising ceremony and exchanged songs and salutes with their Italian friends, who named this third camp, Independence Camp in honor of the day.

On July 5, the Duke split the Americans into two detachments of five men each. These two groups would use a relay system to ferry loads of supplies from the camp on the Malaspina to the next camp, thereby guaranteeing that the maximum amount of material would be available to the lead party.

It took another four days to cross Pinnacle Pass. Then the party turned their attention toward the Seward plateau, one of the largest glacier masses in the world, nearly 6 miles (10 kilometers) wide and 40 miles (64 kilometers) long. In the mist beyond the jumbled blocks of ice, seracs, and thousands of crevasses rose the summit of Mount Saint Elias.

Now the men had to haul the heavily laden sledges across the Seward Glacier, the most difficult passage so far. Their path doubled back and forth across what had initially appeared to be the shortest route across the glacier, but their zigzag course ended up covering much more than six miles. It took every man helping to pull sledges over the most difficult stretch of the glacier, now burning hot under an oppressive sun. Even the Duke himself took up harness to speed the pace.

The necessity of lessening the load on the sledges had forced Sella to leave his heavy camera obscura at Camp 2 on the Malaspina Glacier, so he now relied on the Ross camera and a smaller experimental Kodak camera that allowed him to focus on something as small as a thicket of dwarf shrubs or a dark blue flowering lupine on a rock wall.

At one point, taking advantage of a rare clear day, Sella took photographs even as he led a route across the glacier. Whenever there was a break in the clouds, he would grab the chance to set up his larger equipment and photograph the surrounding peaks.

Sella spent much of his time fighting the elements. The harsh weather made it virtually impossible to keep the cameras, films, and chemicals stable. Furthermore, the fluctuation between the freezing cold outside and the humidity within the black tent he used as a darkroom affected his equipment, especially his Ross camera. Dozens of prints, including several important panoramas, were ruined when condensation from his own breath gathered on the Rivel gelatin paper he used to develop his shots. Fifty years later, Sella still regretted the loss of those photos.

For the better part of the expedition, Sella and his assistant suffered in silence, patiently waiting in the cold and trying to keep the camera equipment from freezing over. If Sella was lucky enough to get a shot, he had to return to the black tent and spend hours taking the utmost care to develop the film. Other than Botta, there was no one with whom he could share his joys and sacrifices. "The prince has not an artistic temperament at all and the beauty of a view does not interest him," Sella candidly noted.

As the Italians moved ahead, the two teams of Americans continued to ferry loads from Camp 2 at the foot of the Malaspina Glacier to the Italians' forward camps, which were, in this manner, kept well stocked with food. This meant the Italians had only to concern themselves with route finding and breaking trail, a luxury the Russell expeditions had not been able to afford.

Whenever one of the American detachments would catch up with the Italians, the Duke would invite them to have tea. "So thoughtful and democratic; the prince is a most lovable fellow," said Ingraham.

By July 10, the expedition had conquered the Seward Glacier to reach Dome Pass and by July 16 had wound its way across the Agassiz Glacier to its main tributary, the Newton Glacier. It had taken the men fifteen days to cover 55 miles (89 kilometers). Here, at the foot of the Newton Glacier (Camp 15), the Duke ordered the sledges abandoned, just as Russell had done at this same point on his two expeditions. The iron bedsteads were also left behind; from now on each of the Italians would carry an eighty-pound load. The next day the expedition set out across the Newton icefall, which was laced with crevasses and plunging seracs on every side. Avalanches roared down incessantly, and it rained continuously. Several times, one of the party fell through a snow bridge with only the load on his back saving him from plunging clear through. The men had to stop again and again to free their companions from their predicament.

By now the strain of enduring poor weather and deep snow, as well as their dread of avalanches, was draining the reserves of the Italians. They admitted among themselves that these were the toughest conditions they had ever faced as climbers.

On the evening of July 17, the Italian guides were returning to Camp 16 on the Newton Glacier after picking up fresh loads from the American relay team when they saw four men climbing somewhat behind them on the Agassiz Glacier. The men shouted to the Italian guides to wait. When they caught up, they introduced themselves as climbers from the Bryant expedition. Giving the Italian guides a letter with instructions to deliver it directly to the Duke, they turned back down the mountain and were soon out of sight.

That night, with the men all crammed into one tent, the Duke read the letter to his anxious men, who expected to learn that Bryant had already claimed the summit. However, Bryant's letter informed the Duke that he and his party had been delayed by the loss of two men (a porter had fallen ill and another man had had to stay behind to take care of him). Bryant went on to say that after getting to within a mile of the Newton Glacier he had found the going too tough and had decided to abandon the climb. He ended the letter wishing the Duke and his party every success.

The Italians, who had not once caught sight of Bryant's men or found any traces of them, felt quite relieved to find they were once again alone in their quest.

Now the men tackled the glacier with renewed vigor. They followed Russell's route, which connected to a second cascade on the glacier, and was just as dangerous as the lower portion. Avalanches and stonefalls swept the men's path, often just before or just after they passed. Fog and snowstorms slowed their progress—at one point they were confined to their tents for three days. When the weather finally cleared, Mount Saint Elias stood directly in front of them. Sella, who had by now become familiar with the mountain's habits, already had his camera ready and snapped a rare picture of the peak in outline. Then just as quickly as the mountain appeared, it was sealed in the mists.

On July 29, after thirteen days on the Newton Glacier, the Italians established Camp 21, at the base of the summit col. Ingraham turned to the Duke and announced: "Five fair days and you will reach the summit." Always circumspect, the Duke did not believe they would ever see any fair weather on this mountain. But on the morning of July 30, the Italians awoke to find the dawn bright and clear, and three roped teams left Camp 21 to climb the col Russell had climbed six years earlier. The col linked

Mount Saint Elias and Mount Newton and offered a direct line to the summit along a long northeast ridge. In contrast to the conditions that beset the unfortunate 1891 Russell expedition, their food was plentiful and the snow was firm enough for them to make excellent progress.

After six hours, the expedition reached the top of the col, some 3,636 feet (1,108 meters) higher than Camp 21. The Duke officially named it the Russell Col in honor of the man who had been first to conquer it.

That afternoon near dusk, from Camp 22 the men could clearly see the blue waters of Yakutat Bay some 62 miles (100 kilometers) away. Here, their yacht *Aggie* would sail to meet them in a short time. Too excited to sleep on the col, the men packed their loads at midnight with Venus shining over the summit of Mount Newton. It had been a rare occurrence to have even two days of clear weather on the entire climb, and the Italians took this as a providential sign that the summit day would be clear.

On July 31, with the summit visible ahead in the first rays of light, the Italians began the ascent, the wind stinging their faces as they climbed. The Duke, Cagni, and the guides Petigax and Maquignaz left on the first rope, with Gonella, Croux, and Botta on the second. Sella, De Filippi, and Pellissier followed on the third rope. By 5:00 A.M., they had passed the last of the rocky crags, but at 15,700 feet (4,785 meters), the Duke called a halt for a short breakfast and to give the men a rest. Only 2,308 feet (704 meters) of climbing separated them from the summit, but several of the party were already suffering from the altitude—headaches, drowsiness, and difficulty in breathing. The men who were most affected were forced to slow their pace. To avoid separating the party, the Duke, who was committed to the idea that everyone should reach the summit, soon called another halt. De Filippi remembered something he had read about sickness at high altitude and smoked a cigarette. Soon after, he was able to breathe regularly, his drowsiness had disappeared, and he was able to continue on.

At 11:00 A.M., the men were briefly elated when they saw a sharp ice pinnacle at the curve of a rounded summit some 150 feet (46 meters) away. With the last of their energy, the Italians staggered wearily up the last gentle slope to the summit.

At 11:55 A.M., the guides Petigax and Maquignaz stood near the summit and moved aside for the Duke, who stepped forward and planted his foot on the summit amidst the hurrahs of the nine other tired men. Unfurling the small green, white, and red flag of Italy on an ice ax, the Duke and his companions gave another hearty shout for Italy and the king. They had made the 5,793-foot (1,766-meter) climb from the Russell Col to the summit in ten and a half hours.

Sella snapped a summit photo, after which the exhausted men began to lie down. The Duke pleaded with them to finish their assigned meteorological and other scientific observations, but for the most part he had to make these himself.

To the east and north he spotted the enormous massif Russell had named Mount Logan, some 20 miles (32 kilometers) away in the Yukon Territory. Looking to the horizon, some 150 miles (241 kilometers) away, the Duke saw a broad summit. Not seeing a name for it on his map, he called it Lucania in remembrance of the ship that had brought the expedition to America. Another conical peak he named Bona after his young second cousin, a little girl born a year before almost to the day on August 1, 1896.

There was little time to celebrate the climb on the summit. After making his scientific observations, the Duke busied himself in trying to rouse his men from their lethargy. Once on their feet, however, the Italians quickly descended the summit, glissading and running wherever possible.

Sella, finding the next day clear, reclimbed the peak from the col with Botta. This time he carried his Ross panoramic camera to 16,400 feet (4,999 meters) in order to take a photo from the northeast crest of the peak. In the excellent weather, it was one of the rare times the camera performed well, and Sella was rewarded with a stunning view of Mount Logan.

On August 3, Ingraham and his porters fought their way up to Camp 21 to reunite with the Italians in heavily falling snow. As Ingraham approached the camp, he shouted to the Italians, "Did you reach the top?" "Yes!" came the reply out of the thick fog and snow. "All of you?" Ingraham asked. "Yes, all of us!" From somewhere out of the mist, the Italians heard Ingraham's men raise a loud hurrah.

Climbers and porters quickly descended the col down the Newton Glacier, taking only two days to traverse a distance that had taken them two weeks to climb. Like horses smelling the barn, the Italians were in a hurry and grew indifferent to keeping their clothes and tents dry.

By now, the snowfields had begun to melt, leaving bare earth with plants in full bloom as the party pushed their lightened sledges across the rocks and gullies. Soon the expedition reached the ice of the Malaspina Glacier. There the sledges often moved so fast that the loads spilled out across the glacier, only to be thrown haphazardly back on the sledge as the men raced to keep up.

On August 10, the party caught sight of Yakutat Bay, where they spied the sails of the *Aggie* coming into harbor. Earlier, Ingraham had foretold the five days of clear weather. Now the Duke reminded him that they were about to meet the *Aggie* at precisely the time the Duke predicted at the beginning of the climb.

The men were elated. They had walked, scrambled, and dragged the sledges over 100 miles (161 kilometers) in fifty-two days, almost always in fog, rain, or snow, and not one accident had occurred, nor had anyone been taken seriously ill. They had committed only one error—in their euphoria at reaching the end of their journey, they had abandoned the sledges on the rocks of the Malaspina and with them their tents. As a result, the entire party was forced to spend a sleepless night on the beach exposed to the hungry mosquitoes.

The next day the ten Italians, Ingraham, and his ten men were still in good cheer as they crammed on deck of the *Aggie* and set sail for Sitka.

Near sunset on the fourth day of sailing, someone caught sight of a cloudlike white peak still visible on the horizon. After a brief debate, everyone agreed it was Mount Saint Elias rising out of the mist, now some 180 miles (290 kilometers) away. As they watched on this clear Alaskan night in calm waters, the summit slowly slipped into the sunset.

Mount Saint Elias receded in popularity as a climbing destination after the turn of the century, when the Himalaya of Tibet and Nepal were opened to Westerners. Its summit was not conquered again until nearly fifty years later, in 1946, when none of the Italians from the 1897 expedition were alive to recount the original ascent.

The peak's poor weather and the logistical difficulties presented by its glaciers continue to challenge climbing parties attempting its summit today. Despite improvement in climbing methods and equipment, the Newton icefall is as treacherous as ever and has claimed several lives. Even today a successful ascent of Mount Saint Elias is a notable achievement.

Chapter Four

ℰ

Farthest North
to the Pole

UPON HIS ARRIVAL IN ITALY AFTER HIS MOUNT SAINT ELIAS EXPEDITION, the Duke received a celebrity's welcome from adoring crowds. Journalists now followed his every move, clamoring for details from the country's first modern hero of exploration. Queen Margherita's gambit had been successful. Italy forgot her troubles and basked in the reflected glow of the Duke's newfound fame.

The Duke's return coincided with a new assignment on board the *San Martino*, a disarmed battleship refitted to serve as a training vessel and anchored in the port of La Spezia.[8] Umberto Cagni was once again assigned as the Duke's staff aide.

One day while reading newspapers published in their absence, Cagni and the Duke came across an article about the ill-fated attempt of Swedish engineer Salomon August Andrée to fly across the North Pole to Alaska in a balloon.

As they talked further, they imagined the possibility of an Italian expedition being the first to reach the Pole, the Holy Grail of exploration. The Duke and Cagni began to strategize their approach much as they would prepare a naval campaign. Gradually a plan took shape.

On their expedition to Mount Saint Elias, they had endured climatic conditions similar to those they might face in the polar regions. Their experience in Alaska had demonstrated that as individuals they had the technical ability and physical endurance that would be needed to conquer the polar pack ice. Furthermore, a polar expedition was essentially a sea voyage, and together they had already planned and executed several long naval voyages.

In February 1898, the Duke and Cagni decided it was time to test their polar theories and left Italy on a private voyage to the Spitsbergen (Svalbard) Islands in the Arctic Ocean. There they undertook long marches on skis and snowshoes and closely questioned elderly sailors who had served on whaling crews. The experienced polar sailors thought the two earnest young men were reckless in their enthusiasm, but the Duke and Cagni returned to Italy feeling they were better prepared than many who had ventured on the pack ice before them.

Back in Turin during the spring and summer of 1898, the Duke turned his attention to editing De Filippi's account of the Mount Saint Elias expedition and consulting with Sella to make the final selection of photographs for the book. Upon seeing Sella's photographs for the first time, the Duke deferred to the great photographer's artistry, saying that his own photographs were "not worthy of staying in a book where there are so many lofty illustrations." The two worked from sunrise until late at night with only three small breaks for meals, the Duke also taking a daily two-hour bicycle ride for exercise. Although flattered at Sella's suggestion that his portrait photograph be used on the book's cover, the Duke insisted that Sella's photograph of Mount Saint Elias would be a more suitable illustration.

After the book's publication in London (in 1900) as *The Ascent of Mount St. Elias*, the Duke wrote Sella that his photographs were "much admired in London." He added that De Filippi was due to travel to London soon to give an account of the expedition. De Filippi's visit, the Duke added with dry wit, would "give us a good indication of what the English lords think of that summit which we have prevented them from deflowering."

The Duke also spent time that summer climbing in the French and Italian Alps. Among the peaks he conquered was the Aiguille Sans Nom ("The Nameless Peak," also known as Aiguille Petigax) in the group of spires known as the Aiguilles of Chamonix high on the Mont Blanc massif. Climbing with Joseph Petigax, Laurent Croux, and Alfred Simond, the Duke ascended the route by the Southeast/East Ridge, a difficult ascent threatened with rockfalls on the lower part.

In June, the Duke journeyed to England to race in the prestigious Harwich Regatta at the Royal Harwich Yacht Club. Summer races between the Prince of Wales's *Britannia* and Kaiser Wilhelm II's *Meteor II* at Cowes, home of the Royal Yacht Squadron near Portsmouth, had popularized the sport among the British and German aristocracy. The heated rivalry between the two yachts soon expanded to an international contest among many of the princes of Europe, who vied for honor with ever larger and faster yachts. Society's finest ladies and gentlemen came to show off their latest fashions at the endless round of parties accompanying the events.

Keen to improve Italy's prestige in Europe, the Duke had joined the rivalry, which he approached with the same ardor that he brought to climbing. Taking advantage of new handicapping rules that gave time allowances for smaller yachts, the Duke approached George L. Watson, the designer of the *Britannia* and the *Meteor II*, to build a small, fast vessel that might be able to win against the larger, heavily favored yachts.

The Duke's new yacht, the eighty-nine-foot-long *Bona*, was commissioned in 1897. During the summer the Duke was away climbing Mount Saint Elias, the *Bona* had dominated the English racing season. Although the *Bona* was never pitted boat-to-boat against the *Britannia* or the *Meteor II*, the little yacht won sixteen races, compared with the *Meteor II*'s thirteen and the *Britannia*'s ten.

In August the Duke was in England again for the race at Cowes. In typical fashion, he chose to sail as a crewman on his yacht rather than to mingle with society. Under the command of its English captain, the *Bona* completed the 1898 season with thirty-nine prize flags, thirty-two of them first places, and three Queen's trophies.

To honor the *Bona*'s crew and skipper for their achievements over the past two racing seasons, the Duke hosted a lavish banquet and dinner dance for the men and their friends at London's Swan Hotel. During the after-dinner toasts, the Duke denied reports that he was commissioning a ninety-foot yacht to race against Sir Henry Lipton's *Shamrock*, Britain's challenger for the 1899 America's Cup. The Duke explained that he had achieved all he desired in yacht racing and that he would now be turning all his attention to leading an expedition to the North Pole.

In October, the *Bona* was pulled ashore and anchored in the mud of an English lagoon. The following May it was sold to an Englishman for £4,000.

Deep in preparations for their North Pole expedition, in September 1898 the Duke and Cagni journeyed to Siberia to acquire sled dogs and test their equipment. After several long excursions via sledge outside Irkutsk, they felt they were ready to vie for the most coveted possession of their age—the North Pole.

Early European exploration of the Arctic had been motivated by a search for a sea route to the Orient—the so-called Northwest Passage through the Arctic islands of North America—and in 1576, the English explorer Sir Martin Frobisher had voyaged as far as the Canadian Arctic. Several other explorers continued the search, including Henry Hudson, but by 1631, after a string of unsuccessful attempts, interest in finding the passage had waned.

It was only after the end of the Napoleonic Wars, when the British navy found itself with an excess of manpower in need of employment, that the search was renewed. In 1818 Lieutenant William Edward Parry undertook the first of several expeditions to the polar region, eventually reaching a latitude of 82°45' north in 1827.

The English navy found it easy to recruit crew and officers alike because polar duty offered rapid advancement through the ranks. The risks, however, were great. Hundreds of men never returned home, losing their lives quickly when their ships sank in the icy waters or dying slowly of starvation or the dreaded scurvy. Soon there were as many voyages organized to look for lost expeditions as there were new ones. After the disappearance of Sir John Franklin's expedition of 1845–1847, fifteen search parties were launched to either rescue or establish the disappearance of Franklin. Finally, in 1859, evidence was found that showed Franklin's men had starved to death.

In 1860, the Royal Geographical Society proclaimed that Franklin had found a Northwest Passage.[9] Future expeditions would focus their efforts on reaching the North Pole. The loss of ships and men continued, however, and by the 1890s it was clear that expeditions were no better equipped to handle the dangers of polar exploration than they had been fifty years before. Iron-hulled steamships were just as likely to be crushed and sent to the bottom of the Arctic Ocean as earlier, wooden-hulled whaling vessels had been. And despite the many advances of medical science, there was still no cure for scurvy, a degenerative disease that could quickly disable a crew.

A new age of polar exploration began on June 24, 1893, when Fridtjof

Nansen set off from Norway to conquer the North Pole. The thirty-two-year-old Nansen, who had led the first expedition across the ice fields of Greenland in 1888, approached the challenge with a new idea: he would not try to force his way through the ice as all previous expeditions had done, but rather let his ship become stuck in the ice off the northeast coast of Siberia and then drift northwest with the polar currents for nearly two years until it was close to the Pole.[10] He would then take dog sledges and travel the rest of the way on foot. To this end, Nansen built the *Fram* ("Forward"), a rugged, squat wooden vessel reinforced with iron and steel and equipped with both sails and a steam engine. The *Fram* was flat-bottomed and flexible to allow it to withstand the pressures of the ice as the expedition wintered in the polar basin.

Nansen's success in Greenland was to a great extent due to his knowledge and emulation of the survival tactics of the Eskimo culture. He learned to speak the Eskimo language and wore Eskimo garments made from the fur of seals and polar bears, which provided more warmth and were less likely to freeze than wool garments. He adopted the Eskimo-style of sledge, which was lighter and more flexible than its Norwegian counterpart. Learning that the Eskimo never suffered from scurvy, apparently because their diet of raw meat provided the nutrients lacking in preserved food, he became adept at hunting polar bears and seals. He also introduced the Norwegian ski (which is much like today's cross-country ski) as a way for men to travel quickly across the ice.

Nansen's method of crew selection also departed from established style. Instead of men suited to serving within the typical naval hierarchy of the British expeditions, he looked for men with the temperament to withstand two or three years of monotonous isolation without going mad. In Nansen's view, only Norwegian sailors with experience on whaling ships were capable of that challenge.

Letting the *Fram* settle into the polar ice in September 1893, Nansen and his crew, headed by Captain Otto Sverdrup, drifted for almost eighteen months, by which time the polar currents had brought them to about 84° north latitude. On March 14, 1895, Nansen set out from the *Fram* with one companion, F. Hjalmar Johansen, with dog sledges and skis, and on April 18, the two Norwegians reached 86°14' north, the northernmost latitude yet attained by any expedition.

Having set their record, Nansen and Johansen spent the next fourteen months struggling first to reach land and then to survive the winter. On June 17, 1896, while traveling along the coast of Franz Josef Land, they literally stumbled upon the English polar explorer Frederick George Jackson, who himself was looking for a route through the ice. Their long journey was ended.

In a period of thirty-five months Nansen had covered a total distance of more than 700 miles (1,127 kilometers). Yet for all the accomplishments of this remarkable three-year journey, he had advanced less than 3° farther north than Parry's expedition sixty-eight years before.

Impressed by Nansen's accomplishment, the Duke journeyed to Norway to seek his advice. After expressing his admiration, the Duke told Nansen he hoped to surpass the explorer's farthest north record. Nansen, impressed by the young Italian's bravado, offered his support.

In planning his expedition the Duke would adopt many of Nansen's ideas, but he rejected the idea of spending more than one winter sealed in the pack ice. He decided to follow Nansen's route by sailing as far north as possible to Franz Josef Land. There, he would journey along the coastline to a point where the vessel could winter at a latitude of 82° north. From there, the Italian expedition would set out on foot and by sledge, traveling across the pack ice in the summer months, from mid-March to mid-May. Prior to March, it would be too dark to travel. After the middle of May, the ice would be broken up and too soft to cross safely.

The Duke believed that the entire journey of more than 1,200 miles (1,931 kilometers) could be made within the allotted ninety-day period, even allowing for drifting pack ice, accidents, and bad weather. His estimates were based on Robert Edwin Peary's figures from his 1892 Greenland expedition; the American explorer claimed he had traveled 1,100 miles (1,770 kilometers) in eighty-five days, or about 13 miles (21 kilometers) per day. It is not known whether the Duke took into consideration that Peary's estimates were based on travel along the Greenland coastline, which is part of the polar ice cap and much easier to travel on than pack ice.

The Duke noted, however, that Peary's figures contrasted sharply with those of Nansen, who had averaged only 5.5 miles (8.9 kilometers) per day over some 700 miles (1,127 kilometers). The Duke reasoned he could match Peary's pace by taking a larger team of men and dogs.

With the idea of Italy being the first to reach the Pole on every Italian's lips, the Duke had little trouble convincing his uncle, King Umberto, to fund yet another expedition.

For his ship, the Duke bought the *Jason*, which had carried Nansen on his 1893–1896 Greenland expeditions. Built at Sandefjord in 1881, this three-masted whaler was also equipped with an auxiliary 60-horsepower steam engine. It weighed 570 tons, measured 131 feet by 30 feet at its widest, and was capable of making 7 knots. The Duke had modifications made to the ship's masts and its hull as well as to its interior. Whereas previous polar expeditions had built stone or wood huts for their base camps, the Duke decided to refit the *Jason* so it could house the expedition comfortably during the winter—a decision that would later have near-disastrous consequences. A full carpenter's shop was also built on deck along with a darkroom, featuring the latest in equipment. Because the object of the expedition was to get as near as possible to the zenith of a star known to all sailors as the Polar Star, the Duke renamed the ship the *Stella Polare* (*Polar Star*).

Nansen's influence was apparent in the Duke's choice of a mixed crew of Norwegian and Italian sailors under the command of C. Julius Evensen, a Norwegian whaling captain familiar with Arctic waters. Each was chosen on the basis of his being able to share in all tasks, from cooking and hunting to navigating across the ice if necessary.

Like Nansen, the Duke understood that Arctic expeditions based on a military-style hierarchy were often too rigid to accommodate the many surprises the journey might present. Military command more often than not broke down during times of hardship and isolation. He needed an expedition team that depended more on camaraderie and mutual support than on strict military protocol. He put special emphasis on hiring men who would be agreeable to each other in times of stress.

In keeping with his egalitarian character, the Duke commented in the preface to the book about the expedition: "If the men were all equally well treated, a good understanding between men on the ship would not be disturbed."

While the *Polar Star* was being refitted in Norway, the Duke returned to his family home in Turin, where he interviewed many potential expedition participants, among them a forty-two-year-old priest by the name of Achille

Ratti. Despite Ratti's alpine achievements in the Monte Rosa region, the Duke decided not to hire him because he was concerned that the presence of a priest would dampen the spirits of his rough crew, who should at least be allowed the use of profane language as a release for tension. (Twenty-three years later, in 1922, Ratti would become Pope Pius XI, a progressive pope known for ardently fostering the rights of workers and the oneness of mankind.)

As finally constituted, the twenty-man expedition was a youthful one. Besides the Duke, now twenty-six, it included the thirty-six-year-old Cagni as the Duke's second in command. Lieutenant Francesco Querini, thirty-one, served as Cagni's aide, and Dr. Achille Cavalli Molinelli, thirty-three, served as the ship's doctor. The senior man aboard was Evensen, the forty-seven-year-old Norwegian captain.

Joseph Petigax, thirty-eight, was again chief guide, as he had been on the Mount Saint Elias expedition. Three other Val d'Aosta guides were also included: Félix Ollier, thirty, who had climbed the Southwest Face of the Grandes Jorasses with the Duke in 1896; Ciprien Savoie, thirty; and Alexis Fenoillet, thirty-seven.

In addition to eight Norwegian seamen, the crew included two Italian sailors: Giacomo Cardenti and Simone Canepa. Last, but not least, was Gino Gini, the cook, who stocked an ample kitchen with wine, pasta, and a variety of delicacies. From his naval voyages, the Duke well understood that good food meant good morale.

On May 7, 1899, the Duke and his Italian team met with King Umberto at the Quirinal Palace in Rome, where the king honored the explorers in a farewell celebration. It would be the last time the Duke would see his uncle alive.

When the Italians arrived in Norway in early June, the last of the provisions—enough for four years—and equipment, including sledges designed by Nansen, heavy clothing, and warm bedding, had been loaded on the *Polar Star*, which had left the shipyard in Larvik on May 28 and was headed for Christiania (Oslo). While they waited for the ship to arrive Nansen invited the Duke and his crew to his estate in Lijsken to celebrate their departure.

The Duke and Nansen had worked closely together for months, poring over maps and plans. Now, walking together under the bright northern sky, they discussed last-minute details late into the night. Inside the house, the

Italians danced and sang with the Norwegians who would be their companions for many months.

The King of Sweden telegraphed his best wishes for success to Nansen's estate, and the next day, after the Italians had returned to Christiania, the Duke's eldest brother, Emanuele Filiberto, the Duke of Aosta, and his wife, Hélène, arrived to say their good-byes. On June 12, a crowd of well-wishers stood on shore watching as the tiny *Polar Star*, bedecked with flags, motored out of the harbor. A full naval salute was fired by large guns at the nearby military fort.

On June 30, the men of the *Polar Star* looked over the sides of the ship and saw their first signs of floating ice as they entered the Russian port of Archangel. Here they were greeted by the Russian dog trader, Alexander Trontheim, who was waiting for them with 121 dogs.

To the Duke's consternation, the dogs Trontheim had chosen looked as if they had suffered badly in their 1,100-mile (1,770-kilometer) journey from Siberia. They were small, thin, and smelly, and their hair was matted. They fought constantly amongst themselves, looked anything but tough, and barked nonstop. The journey had not even begun and the Duke wondered if he had made a huge mistake.

On July 3, an Italian delegation led by Count Oldofredi brought presents from Queen Margherita and the Duke's sister-in-law and then attended a brief prayer ceremony with their compatriots amidst the howling dogs. The Italian ambassador and Grand Duke Vladimir, brother of the Czar, also visited the ship to extend their best wishes. On July 12, the *Polar Star* left Archangel to a naval gun salute from the Russians and headed due north for Franz Josef Land.

Unbeknownst to the Duke, three other expeditions had already set sail for the North Pole that same month, one led by Peary from Grant Land (Ellesmere Island); another led by Otto Sverdrup, the captain of Nansen's *Fram*, from Greenland; and a third led by the American journalist and explorer Walter Wellman, from Franz Josef Land.

The *Polar Star* reached Franz Josef Land without much difficulty at latitude 72° north and steered to Cape Flora, the westernmost point of Northbrook Island. Here they stored eight months' worth of provisions as an emergency cache. They then headed west toward Cape Crowther, and the Italian crew got their first taste of sailing amid the pack ice.

Near Bruce Island, the *Polar Star* became caught in the grip of ice 30 feet thick. Hemmed in by hummocks of ice two stories high, the ship remained stuck fast while its hull, under immense pressure, creaked and groaned, drowning all conversation. The men tried to remain calm, despite the fact the vessel had heeled over to an angle of 6 degrees.

When the Duke climbed to the crow's nest for a better view of their surroundings, he saw the masts of a whaler sailing far ahead in open water. The news created a wave of humiliation among the crew, who were not used to being bested by a whaling ship.

After days of blasting with dynamite and reversing the engines back and forth, Evensen finally freed the ship and reached open water.

"What a strange land," the Duke wrote in his journal. "We ceaselessly pass from hopes to delusions and from delusions to hopes."

The *Polar Star* was slowly making its way north when it came upon Wellman's *Capella*, returning with an injured Wellman on board. A pressure ridge had damaged his ship, killing dogs and ruining their sledges.

The crews called to out to each other as the ships passed, sailing in different directions. It would be the *Polar Star's* last sight of civilization for many months.

On August 6, the ship sailed north through the open waters of the British Channel, steering for Cape Fligely, the northernmost extremity of Prince Rudolph Island. On August 16, 1899, thirty-six days after leaving Archangel, the expedition reached the island, where the Duke chose a winter anchorage in Teplitz Bay at a latitude of 80°47' north.

The small bay was surrounded on two sides by tall rocky walls and nearly covered by a sheet of ice, but Captain Evensen skillfully guided the *Polar Star* through an open channel and anchored flush against the walls of the ice field. The Duke theorized that this sheltered location would protect the vessel throughout the winter. Most Arctic disasters were the result of ships' being crushed by the pack ice.

With the *Polar Star* ready for winter camp, the men fell into a daily routine that they would follow for the next six months. Working in cozy dens below decks, the men prepared the materials needed to build storage huts on the beach as well as kennels for the dogs. The Duke started work on his scientific studies.

Late on September 7, the crew was awakened by the noise of gale-force winds outside the ship and a sound they had never heard before—the crashing of huge ice ridges against the rocks of the cape. Without warning, the *Polar Star* suddenly pitched over, spilling the crew and their possessions onto the decks.

The first men on deck could see by the dim light that a pressure ridge nearly 20 feet high had heaved up past the ice field and now threatened to sink the ship. As they watched in horror, the bow of the *Polar Star* rose completely out of the water and heeled over to an angle of 20 degrees. The rigging of the foremast had broken loose in the tempest, and the engineers shouted that water was rising quickly in the engine room. Outside, the wind rose in its fury.

Rousted from their sleep, the men quickly tried to dress in the chaos below decks. The Duke, scrambling to put on his clothes, ordered them to begin taking provisions off the boat before it sunk. The best they could manage was a few loads at a time as they slipped and fell on the slanted ice-covered decks. Cagni, working by lantern light, worked frantically below, trying to install makeshift hand pumps to keep the sea water from reaching the engines, whose boilers would crack if they came in contact with it. "There rose in my mind," the Duke later wrote," involuntary recollections of unfortunate expeditions."

Believing that the ship would soon sink, the Duke ordered the Italian flag hoisted, and from shore the crew watched helplessly, expecting the *Polar Star* to slip below the surface at any moment.

But the *Polar Star* did not sink. Although she had a gap in her planks as wide as a hand, the ice had frozen the vessel in place with the hull out of the water. When Cagni examined the damage, he found that not only was everything inside covered with ice but nearly every part of the ship's structure, including the deck beams and frame timbers, had been dislocated and that the propeller shaft was bent. But despite the damage, there was still time to save the ship. As long as the weather remained cold, the ship would remain stuck in ice nearly 2 feet thick.

Among the ship's provisions were air pumps that had been brought to inflate small dirigibles intended to help move the sledges across the ice. Cagni quickly put the pumps to a new purpose. He ordered the crew to melt the ice inside the ship and begin pumping the water from the *Polar Star*. Fortunately, the engines had not been destroyed, and the ship appeared to be repairable.

In the end, however, the vessel had to be abandoned. The tilt of its decks made it uninhabitable, which was a great disappointment to the Duke, who had so carefully planned the *Polar Star*'s transformation into a comfortable winter residence for the expedition party.

Having done all he could do below decks, the indefatigable Cagni, who possessed a ceaseless optimism throughout the ordeal, ordered the men to set up a makeshift camp. He designed field tents using the ship's sails, and in a few days, the men had built two large shelters, one for the nine Norwegians and another for the eleven Italians.

With their lives remarkably changed, camp life assumed a new routine. The men were required to arise at 7:00 A.M., eat a hearty breakfast at 8:00, and go to work on the ship at 9:00. After a full day of exhausting repair work, the men would meet again at 6:30 for dinner. The Duke took note that the routine was much like military school, and the men, robbed of their privacy, kept to themselves and spoke little, anxious not to disrupt the fragile social balance.

Despite having a large supply of books, the men had little time to read. During the day, in the feeble light of the Arctic autumn, they worked on the ship in temperatures of -22 degrees Fahrenheit (-30 degrees Celsius). By night, they worked to improve their fragile tents, improvising vents so they would not suffocate from the smoke of their stoves.

The Duke, Cagni, and Lieutenant Querini also kept busy hunting, shooting polar bears and an occasional seal or walrus, which provided the party with fresh meat. Housed in hastily built kennels on the ice, the dogs barked incessantly and if left too long on their own fought ferociously among themselves. As the Duke later wrote, "They feared nothing except water and the whip."

On November 4, a severe Arctic storm hit the camp and continued unabated for nine days, shaking the tent beams so fiercely that they groaned. The men, worried they would lose their newfound homes, sat in silence, unable to speak to one another above the winds, watching the barometer for any sign that would indicate a break in the storm. After the storm, the men emerged to find their world had become dark and silent. For the rest of the Arctic winter, work would have to be conducted by the light of their oil lamps.

The crew's grim routine was temporarily broken on Queen Margherita's birthday in late November, when the Duke brought out the gifts Margherita and his sister-in-law Hélène had sent to the ship before it left Archangel. As the men opened the various small trinkets, the touching remembrances brought tears to their eyes. Now, as never before, they began to feel their isolation and despair. Instead of making them happy, the presents nearly destroyed their morale.

After three months at Teplitz Bay, most of which had been spent on repairs of one sort or another, the Duke decided to halt work on the *Polar Star*. The decision cheered the beleaguered men, who had signed on as explorers, not as carpenters.

Relieved from their duties and somewhat assured that the *Polar Star* would not sink, the men began to discuss their plans for an assault on the Pole. Immediately, their spirits rose as they talked excitedly about preparing their sledges and taking the dogs out for training runs. They would venture out on the ice as soon as the winds had calmed and temperatures rose.

On December 23, with temperatures warming to 28 degrees Fahrenheit (-2 degrees Celsius), the Duke, Cagni, and Petigax each took a dog team and sledge to the end of the bay, where the snow was good, and raced off across the ice. Caught up in the exhilaration of skimming across the smooth surface, they imagined the journey to the Pole would be just as thrilling and swift. Soon however, the wind began to blow, and temperatures fell to -4 degrees Fahrenheit (-20 degrees Celsius). Petigax, in the lead, was soon lost to sight in the enveloping mist. Suddenly, in front of the Duke and Cagni appeared a steep drop-off. Before they could react, their sledges plunged over the brink, crashing some 30 feet below.

The two men pulled themselves from the wreckage unhurt, but, enveloped in darkness, they did not know which way to go. Their shouts soon brought Petigax racing back toward them with a lantern. One dog was injured and had to be destroyed, and the two sledges were damaged (they would later be retrieved). By the time the men had made their way back up the long slope, the wind had died down, but they were lost. At one point the sky cleared briefly and they were able to recognize a star by which to orient themselves. Finally, they heard a distant bell being rung by their worried comrades and followed its sound to camp.

Two days later, Christmas Day, as he tried to make a display from the men's wrapped gifts, the Duke noticed that something was wrong with his hands. Soon his fingers blistered. On New Year's Day, the men fired rockets and guns to celebrate the new century, but the Duke was in so much pain that he had to limit himself to a few simple tasks.

On January 15, Molinelli, the expedition doctor, amputated the first joint of the Duke's middle finger and the ends of the first and little fingers on his left hand. Later, Molinelli would also have to cut away part of the fourth finger. As a result, the Duke could not even put on his own clothes without help.

Finally, on January 29, the Duke's twenty-seventh birthday, he gave command of the expedition to Cagni, whose own fingers were hurting. Despite the setbacks, Cagni gave the order that the expedition would go ahead as planned.

Cagni and the Duke had previously devised a pyramid-style expedition. Three detachments would carry enough supplies to feed the entire expedition until it reached the 85th parallel. Here, the first detachment would return to camp. At the 88th parallel, the second detachment would return, leaving the third with enough dogs and provisions to go on to the Pole and return. The detachment would use a total of 13 sledges, each carrying 671 pounds, and 104 dogs.

On February 21, 1900, the three teams of four men each lined up their sledges and stood ready to set out for the Pole. The Duke, with tears in his eyes and his left hand in a sling, led them in salutes of "Long live the King!" and the expedition departed. The Duke stood for a long time watching them disappear into the polar twilight.

Returning to his tent, the Duke spent the next two days sitting on his cot in somber silence. By now the temperature had fallen to -45 degrees Fahrenheit (-43 degrees Celsius), and from far away could be heard the sound of the ice crashing against the coast. Near the end of the third day, he thought he heard the distant sound of dogs barking and went outside to investigate. On the far horizon, he could see the men and sledges of the expedition returning.

When they arrived in camp, the Duke discovered that Cagni had fallen through the ice. He had been pulled free, but his clothes were frozen from head to foot, and his hands were severely frostbitten. Once in camp, Cagni revived considerably and explained that the extreme drop in temperature and the low light had made travel very difficult. Then a dog had died, and one of Ollier's toes had frozen. Eversen and several men also began to show the effects of frostbite, and Cagni had given the order to turn back. Although the first attempt had gone badly, Cagni felt that if certain improvements were made they could try again and still make it back by May 20, before the snow became too soft to travel.

To reduce the amount of food and equipment needed for the journey, Cagni cut back the number of men from twelve to ten. The group now included Cagni, Querini, Molinelli, Canepa, Cardenti, Petigax, Fenoillet, Ollier, Savoie, and one of the Norwegian seamen, the ship's chief engineer, Henrik Stökken, who had frequently requested permission to go.

Cagni also had the men trade their heavy sealskin parkas for wool clothing. The fur had made the fast-moving men pour sweat, which then froze and rubbed their backs raw against the tough hides. They also stuffed their reindeer-hide boots with *finnesko* (dried moss) to help keep their feet drier and thus warmer.

With 102 dogs pulling thirteen sledges, each carrying 551 pounds, the three detachments set off once again on Sunday, March 11, in relatively mild temperatures of -1 degree Fahrenheit (-18.3 degrees Celsius).

The Duke, who still had trouble dressing himself and felt pain whenever exposed to the cold, escorted the expedition out to the pack ice. Climbing with some difficulty to a high pressure ridge, he watched his companions depart and finally disappear against the white horizon. On his way back to camp, distracted in contemplating his despair, the Duke fell into a shallow pool of water and, even more depressed, had to be cut out of his frozen clothes.

Remaining at camp with the Duke were Captain Evensen, the seven other Norwegians, and the Italian cook Gini. Crippled with pain and having few people to converse with, the Duke was left to listen to the never-ending crunching of the pack ice, the occasional dog barking, and the sound of the cook's gun as he took a shot at an encroaching polar bear.

Out on the ice, Cagni was not enjoying the swift journey he had hoped for. Instead of making 12 or more miles (19 or more kilometers) a day as they had believed they would, their progress had slowed to a crawl. With just seventy-two days in which to reach the Pole and return (an estimated distance of 1,200 miles [1,931 kilometers] round trip), Cagni saw they were making less than half the daily mileage needed. The dream of reaching the Pole began to slip from their grasp. Every two hundred steps, they had to stop and carve a route through the massive ice hummocks, while the sea ice often shifted, opening large cracks around which they had to detour. Furthermore, the ice floes on which they traveled would frequently shift direction, with the result that even though they had marched all day they might have gained only a foot in latitude. Each operation was slow and complicated because of the cold. Worry about their lack of speed only added to their fatigue.

Dinner hour, which they once had looked forward to with some pleasure, now became a time of despair. At day's end, the ten men would set up the frozen tent, start the gas stoves for cooking, feed the dogs, clean their boots, and finally manage to eat something themselves, if they could down a few sips of soup before it froze to the mess tin. Then, in silence, they crawled into their frozen sleeping bags, which had become as hard as wood. With temperatures falling to -52 degrees Fahrenheit (-47 degrees C), they were lucky to get a few hours' sleep each night.

The pedometer wheels they brought along to measure their progress had broken, but the men already knew that it was pointless to calculate their speed. The pressure ridges were deceptively treacherous to cross, and the open-water channels opened and closed with startling speed. Cagni's fingers still burned in pain from his earlier frostbite, and Ollier, whose toe had recovered, now developed a frostbitten heel.

Given his men's condition, Cagni decided to send back the first detachment two days early, on March 21. He chose his aide, Lieutenant Querini, whose endurance was failing, to command the detachment. Ollier was sent back because of his frostbitten foot, and Stökken because his inability to speak Italian was proving troublesome. They would take three sledges and enough food for twelve days.

Setting their direction, Cagni pointed to the outline of Prince Rudolph Island some 45 miles (73 kilometers) away, telling Querini to head for it in a southeasterly direction, following the expedition's original trail, which had been well marked.

The topography of the ice was in constant change, and the day after the detachment's departure, Cagni had the horrible thought that perhaps the pack ice had turned on itself and was now heading back south. His hands had been so badly numbed that he had been unable to take a sextant reading, and he now feared he had misidentified Prince Rudolph Island the day before. He only hoped that Querini could make any necessary adjustments.

The next few days were cloudy and much colder as the remaining two detachments continued across the giant ice hummocks. March 30 dawned in clear weather. Cagni's hands had healed enough that he was able to take a reading, and he found that the expedition had reached a latitude of 83°16' north. He now sent back the second detachment, consisting of Molinelli in command, Cardenti, and Savoie, three sledges, a kayak, and enough rations to last eighteen days. Cagni told Molinelli, as he had Querini, to head as much as possible toward the southeast and not to alter course unless absolutely necessary.

Five days after leaving Cagni, Molinelli's second detachment had covered less than 20 miles (32 kilometers). Fog and a stiff wind from the west had prevented Molinelli from taking a sextant reading to locate their course. It was impossible to camp on level ground because of the shifting pack ice, and at one point, the men were pinned in by pressure ridges on every side. They could stay in one spot no longer than two or three hours before breaking camp to find a safer haven. At night they kept their ears pressed to the ground to listen for warnings that the ice was breaking up.

After ten days of poor weather, sleeplessness, and many detours, they saw land, but being unable to take a reading they were still lost. They pushed on in falling snow and drifting pack ice, and on April 12 found themselves out of pemmican for the dogs. They knew that from now on, they would have to kill a dog each day in order to feed the remaining animals.

On April 15, Easter Sunday, Molinelli was able to take a reading and decided they were near Cape Germania and the Karl Alexander Islands. In celebration of their good fortune, the men made up their last ration of tea, but in their giddiness at being close to home, Cardenti mistakenly put salt instead of sugar into the pot. The bitter-tasting tea was an ominous sign of things to come.

Two days later, the three men sighted land a half mile (0.8 kilometer) away. Uncertain of where exactly they were, but sure they could reach land the next morning, they decided to eat the last of their food. However, in the night the current took them out to sea again, and they drifted to the northwest. In the morning, they discovered that they were now some 6 miles (10 kilometers) from land. An anxious Molinelli ordered Cardenti to take the kayak and go for help across the open sea.

Back in the camp at Teplitz Bay, the Duke was looking forward to the return of the first detachment and on March 20 had gone to Cape Fligely, expecting to meet them. He scanned the horizon with a telescope all day and stood watch again the next day for as long as he could bear the wind burning his still-painful left hand.

So that he could continue his vigil out of the wind, the Duke ordered the construction of an igloo on top of a 300-foot ridge at the cape. For days he sat alone, confined to a small tent placed within the igloo. To keep warm he added a lantern and cookstove, which filled the cramped space with smoke.

On April 15, the Duke left Cape Fligely disappointed and returned to Teplitz Bay to celebrate Easter Sunday. At services that day, the rest of the men were similarly distressed, and the occasion was passed in silence and sadness. The Duke feared the worst.

Three days later, as the Duke sat in camp contemplating the loss of his men, he heard yelling in the distance and soon the dogs began to bark. Then someone yelled, "Cardenti is back!"

Cardenti had crossed the 6 miles (10 kilometers) of ocean to Prince Rudolph Island with some difficulty. Forced by the current to land his kayak near an icefall, he had spent several hours climbing through crevasses to the top of a ridge and the rest of the night walking to the camp. Several men left camp immediately to find Molinelli and Savoie and ferry them by kayak back to the island.

The Duke rejoiced at the news that Molinelli, Cardenti, and Savoie had returned, but was shocked to realize he was meeting the second detachment, not the first.

Cardenti was carrying a letter from Cagni saying that the first detachment, led by Querini, should have reached Prince Rudolph Island, only some 45 miles (73 kilometers) away from their starting point, on April 2. Despite their difficulties, Molinelli's second detachment had traveled 89 miles (143 kilometers) in sixteen days, averaging 5.6 miles (9 kilometers) a day. It then occurred to everyone that Querini could have mistaken White Island to the east for Prince Rudolph Island. The Duke immediately organized a rescue mission of Norwegians to search for the missing men.

Meanwhile, the third detachment, made up of Cagni, Petigax, Canepa, and Fenoillet, had steadily increased their daily speed to nearly 18 miles (30 kilometers) a day across the level ice. On April 17, their thirty-eighth day out on the ice, they crossed the 85th parallel.

Slightly before noon on April 25, Cagni called a halt to take a reading on his sextant and found they had reached a latitude of 86°34', thus establishing a new farthest-north mark. They had exceeded Nansen's record by 23 miles (37 kilometers).

After a brief celebration to share a cognac punch and raise a small Italian flag to salute the Duke and the King, the men pounded three metal pipes into the ice to mark the spot. Into one of these Cagni inserted the message: *April 25, 1900. 86°34' lat. 68° long. east of Greenwich.* "We have reached the end of all our fatigues," he recorded in his diary.

Cagni then took stock of their situation. By his estimate, the men had only enough provisions for thirty days, plus two hundred rations of pemmican for the remaining thirty-four dogs (a mixture of powdered beef and suet, in dire circumstances the pemmican could also provide nourishment for the men). With careful planning, and assuming an average day's journey covered 12 miles (19 kilometers), these supplies should be sufficient for the return journey (both dogs and men would get full rations for more than 12 miles [more than 19 kilometers] traveled per day and half rations for less).

As the men started back, Petigax, who had labored long and hard through the pressure ridges on the way north, was struck by snow blindness. Cagni treated his eyes with a cocaine-based ointment that temporarily helped the uncomplaining guide, but Petigax found it difficult to keep the same pace as before. Even with Petigax's problems, the party still managed to cover 90 miles (145 kilometers) in the first six days.

On May 10, just as it looked as if the return journey was in hand, Cagni discovered that they had deviated from their course to the west and needed to cover another 25 miles (40 kilometers) to reach Teplitz Bay. The men, now weary from twelve-hour marches, talked only of miles. Their once feverish desire for the Pole was now replaced by delirium, and at night they fell asleep before finishing their food.

Cagni's right forefinger had become so badly blistered from frostbite that he had to start cutting away the rotting parts of it himself, piece by piece, at each night's stop. He became feverish with pain and in his anxiety was unable to determine their location.

On May 23, after twenty-eight consecutive days of cloudy weather, snow, fog, and wind, the sun shone briefly. Cagni took a reading and discovered that they were still 40 miles (64 kilometers) west of Prince Rudolph Island, with very little food left, even though the men had been consuming the pemmican intended for the dogs as their situation became more desperate. At night Cagni lay awake, remembering all the Arctic disasters he had heard about and thinking how he would break the bad news to the men. They would have to make forced marches, giving up their precious tea and coffee to save fuel, and they would have to start killing the dogs to feed themselves as well as the other dogs. Not only was the killing a nauseating task for the already depressed men, it was no honor to kill the loyal beasts who had so devotedly pulled the sledges on this seemingly endless journey.

As the men moved east toward Cape Fligely, the temperatures increased to -10 degrees Fahrenheit (-23 degrees Celsius), which softened the snow and made it even more difficult to pull the sledges. This warming also caused the pack ice to break up, creating wide channels of open water. They either had to detour around these or clamber onto ice floes and ferry themselves across—a dangerous maneuver. The men almost lost what resolve they had left when they found they had made less than a thousand yards (900 meters) over a twelve-hour period.

By June 4, the party was out of fuel and water. There was no game of any sort to shoot, not even a bird. On June 8, Fenoillet became snow-blind. That evening the men ate dog's legs, cooked with the last of their butter and salt. Afterwards they chewed coffee grounds to get rid of the taste of the greasy meat.

Delirious and burning with thirst, they made their way east a few feet at a time. With no butter left, they had to use dog fat to cook the dog meat. To kill the taste of dog, they drank warm sea water mixed with a pinch of dried milk. By June 14 they were down to nine dogs, the fewest number that could pull the remaining sledge. Nine days later, having slaughtered two more dogs, they were subsisting on a thin soup of water and bones. In despair, they were huddled in their tent when Fenoillet, who had recovered his sight, suddenly realized that the fog had lifted and took a look outside. He could scarcely believe his eyes. There in front of them, just a few miles away, was the outline of Prince Rudolph Island.

Life in the Teplitz Bay camp since the return of Molinelli had been full of worry. The Norwegian rescue mission had returned on May 10 with no news of the missing men of the first detachment. As the day set for Cagni's return, May 20, passed, the Duke was sure he, too, was in trouble.

Day after day, the men took turns at the Cape Fligely igloo, looking north and watching the sea open and close against the island. With the warmer weather, the pack ice was now miles away, leaving a clear channel between it and the island. There was no way to mount another rescue party.

On June 10, the Duke relieved Molinelli at Cape Fligely and for the next thirteen days kept watch with Cardenti. On June 23, they heard the distant sound of dogs barking. Neither responded immediately because, by now, they had grown used to the camp dogs barking at polar bears. Seeing nothing to the north, the direction from which he expected the detachment to return, the Duke began to search the horizon with his telescope. Finally, far to the west on the edge of the island he caught sight of a single sledge pulled by seven dogs and four men. Having traveled 637 miles (1,025 kilometers) in 104 days, Cagni and his men had returned (a journey intended to take 72 days had lasted more than a month longer).

Considering the deprivation they had undergone, the four men of Cagni's detachment were in remarkably good health. The only casualty was Cagni's finger, which was so damaged that Molinelli had to amputate it.

For the rest of June and all of July, the men had little time to recuperate. None of them wanted to spend another winter on the ice, and they worked long, hard shifts around the clock to finish the repairs on the *Polar Star* and free it from the ice. Open water lay just 540 feet (165 meters) ahead of the ship, but to reach it, the men would have to chop a canal through nearly 20 feet (6 meters) of ice. After weeks of hard work, they had gained only a few feet. Unless they found another way to free the vessel, it was clear that they would have to spend the winter in Teplitz Bay.

Turning from digging the ice out by hand, the men tried explosives. But after numerous blasts, the ice still had not broken up enough for the ship to reach open water. On August 8, they were down to their last mine and their last five detonators. The men held their collective breath as the fuses were lit and waited in silence. Finally there was a great rumbling under the ice. A few seconds later the entire ice sheet fractured, and the *Polar Star* righted itself in the water. The men were too exhausted to cheer.

At last, on August 16, the ship was loaded and steamed away at a steady six knots from Teplitz Bay, the expedition's home for the last twelve months. But their troubles were not over.

For the next two weeks, the *Polar Star* fought its way out of the pack ice, with Captain Evensen maneuvering the ship to avoid the ice floes. At times it seemed that the ship was stuck fast, and the men were gripped by dismay. With no more explosives on board, if the ship could not free itself, they would have to abandon it. Finally, on September 5, the crew stood on deck, watching the last of the broken ice float away in their wake. On the horizon to the south were the mountains of Norway.

That evening, as the *Polar Star* entered Hammerfest harbor, a ship came sailing out to greet them. But the ship bore sad news: the Duke's uncle, King Umberto I, had been assassinated on July 29 by an anarchist's bullet.

When he arrived in Christiania few days later, the Duke was remote and preoccupied as he presided over a solemn torchlight procession of Norwegians paying tribute to the fallen Italian king.

The Duke stayed in Christiania for a month arranging another rescue operation for his three missing men. During this time the Englishman Robert F. Scott, who was preparing for his own polar expedition, came to visit and learn about the details of the Duke's expedition. Apparently, Scott was not impressed. He would later say of their meeting that the Duke had "nice manners," but that "there was not much to be learned [t]here." When Scott finally undertook his epic trip to the South Pole, he ignored the example of the Italian expedition, in which the use of dog teams had played such a crucial role, and relied instead on mechanized tractors and ponies. Tragically, Scott would reach the South Pole a few days after the Norwegian Roald Amundsen, only to perish with four of his comrades in March 1912.

Chapter Five

ੴ

The Ruwenzori
of Africa

HAVING DONE ALL HE COULD IN THE SEARCH FOR HIS MISSING MEN, THE Duke returned to a subdued Rome. After attending the coronation of the new king, his cousin Vittorio Emanuele III, he again, on October 1, 1900, took up his naval duties at La Spezia under a new appointment as *capitano di corvetta*. Because the police believed that he, too, might become the target of assassins, his public appearances were severely limited. Even his private activities were curtailed and he could no longer spontaneously visit his favorite cafes or the opera house. Finally, in January 1901, he resumed his public life, appearing, under close guard, at a meeting of the Italian Geographic Society, where he and Cagni presented the account of the North Pole expedition to the new king and his queen, Elena.

By the summer of 1901, the twenty-eight-year-old Duke was anxious to escape the constraints of his life in the city and so headed to the Alps to climb in the Dames Anglaises group. On August 6, 1901, he left Courmayeur with three veteran guides from the North Pole expedition: Joseph Petigax, Cyprien Savòie, and Alexis Fenoillet. Laurent Croux, who had led the Duke on earlier alpine climbs, was also in the group, along with five porters who carried gear to the foot of the Brenva Glacier and returned to their village before dark.

The party made steady progress up the route, stopping frequently to dodge falling stones. By standing on each other's shoulders, they were able to inch their way up a narrow couloir toward a pinnacle. Near the top, however, they found their way blocked by a smooth overhanging rock face.

They tried to throw a rope over the summit of the pinnacle and pull their way to the top, but the wind blew the rope back in their faces. They then attached a weighted copper ball to the rope and threw it again, still no luck. Finally, they tried launching a rocket to carry the rope over the pinnacle, but the rope drew the rocket off course, and it exploded into the rocks just in front of Croux and Petigax. Deciding safety was the better course, they settled for climbing the second highest pinnacle in the group, which the Duke named Punta Jolanda in honor of the recently born first daughter of Vittorio Emanuele III and Queen Elena.

Describing the climb in the *Alpine Journal,* the Duke suggested that the route to the highest pinnacle "offers a few hours of ticklish gymnastics to those who are fond of scaling steep rock." Should a climber's "agility and acrobatic resources fail him" on an attempt of the pinnacle, he recommended that a "seal gun" be used to shoot the rope over the pinnacle.

Italy at the turn of the century was bustling with modernization. In the north, new industries flourished with the introduction of electricity. Railways were being built to carry food and durable goods across the country. Cities were growing rapidly. And new roads were being built across the country to keep pace with the very latest modern invention: the automobile.

Among the fanatics of automobile travel was Margherita, now the Queen Mother. Umberto Cagni, who was as skilled at fixing automobiles as he was at repairing ship engines, was a passionate and skilled automobile driver and often organized long motor tours to visit his close friend Vittorio Sella in Biella. Not to be outdone, the Duke also became an advocate of the automobile. Typical of his competitive nature, he threw himself into a new form of competition, automobile racing.

The first auto race in Europe, which started in the Duke's home city of Turin and ended in Milan, took place between April 27 and May 11, 1901. That same year, automobile fans across Europe were also captivated by the Tour de France, a 687-mile (1,106-kilometer) race along the winding single-lane pavement from Paris to Berlin.

Yet a third automobile race was to capture Europe's attention that year: Garibaldi Coltelletti, a representative of the French automobile manufacturer Panhard, boasted to the Duke that the twenty-horsepower Panhard could beat the Italian-made, four-cylinder, thirty-horsepower Fiat (an acronym for Fabbrica Italiana di Automobili Torino). In return, the Duke wagered Coltelletti 5,000 lire that his Fiat could beat the Panhard in a 187-mile (301-kilometer) race from Villanova d'Asti to Bologna.

Giovanni Agnelli, the enterprising founder of Fiat in Turin, had the foresight to add to the race another, unofficial, car, which would follow the same route as the Duke and Coltelletti but would start later. According to some reports the driver of this second car was Luigi Storero, while other sources say it was Felice Navarro, who would later become legendary as Fiat's first driver on the international circuit.

On November 24, 1901, amid a crowd of auto enthusiasts and aristocrats, including the Duke's sister-in-law, Hélène, the race began under rain-laden skies and periodic showers. The newly paved roads were slippery.

Coltelletti left the starting line promptly at 8:40, and the Duke, accompanied by Agnelli and a Fiat representative, left fifteen minutes later, with Nazzaro another fifteen minutes behind.

At the 34-mile (55-kilometer) mark, the Duke had cut Coltelletti's lead down to less than ten minutes, and it looked as if the Duke would overtake him.

Outside of Alexandria, the Duke's Fiat was traveling at a speed of between 40 and 50 miles per hour when it skidded out of control on the wet road and struck a kilometer stone near a bridge. The impact broke the car's axle. Dazed but unhurt, the Duke and his companions walked away from the wreck. Coltelletti, who was nearly killed himself when he passed over an unprotected railroad crossing barely ahead of a speeding train, was not aware of the Duke's accident until he reached the finish line seven hours and thirty-four minutes after the race began.

Although the race was won by Coltelletti, Agnelli was pleased. His second driver, Nazzaro, had covered the entire distance in a twelve-horsepower Fiat at an average speed of 22 miles per hour, actually bettering Coltelletti's time by four minutes.

The accident had cured the Duke of any more thoughts of what one wit called "land yachting," but the twenty-nine-year-old prince still had racing in his blood. Early in 1902, he began building another racing yacht to replace the *Bona*. His new yacht, the *Artica*, was designed to compete in the

Coupe de France, the most prestigious yacht race in the Mediterranean. The *Artica* won the race, but the Duke's racing career was cut short: he was about to become a diplomat.

On December 22, 1901, the Duke was promoted to *capitano di fregata*, and in August 1902, he was given command of his first ship, the battle cruiser *Liguria*. His cousin the king, seeing an opportunity to take advantage of Luigi di Savoia's popularity, sent the *Liguria* on a diplomatic tour of the Mediterranean.

The Duke stopped first in Toulon to make a courtesy call on the French admiral. He next made a call in Barcelona, where the Spanish king, Alfonso XIII, invited him to place a crown of flowers at the monument Alfonso had built in memory of the Duke's father, Amedeo di Savoia-Aosta, who had so briefly ruled Spain some thirty years earlier. Finally, he paid a visit to the French fleet stationed at Algiers and Tunis, where he was welcomed and congratulated on his new assignment by French naval officers.

When the *Liguria* returned to La Spezia, the Duke learned that both Germany and Austria, Italy's partners in the Triple Alliance, had been agitated by his visits to the French ports and had reprimanded King Vittorio Emanuele III for the Duke's activities. Although there are no personal records of the incident, it is likely that Vittorio Emanuele passed on the reprimand to the Duke.

Throughout Vittorio Emanuele's reign, the king and the Duke would continue to have difficult encounters. Although they were from the same royal family, the two men were cut from entirely different cloth. In addition, the king may have harbored jealousy toward his cousin, dating as far back as Queen Margherita's closeness to the robust Luigi during Vittorio's sickly childhood.

King Vittorio Emanuele III—unlike Umberto I, his father, and Vittorio Emanuele II, his grandfather—was not a military man. He was, however, better educated in the conduct of politics. He spoke four languages and was an adept, although uneasy, diplomat who disliked public scrutiny. However, because he was short, he was sometimes ridiculed by the press when he appeared in uniform.

In contrast, the Duke was a natural and skilled military officer, who was well liked in the European capitals. He was splendid in uniform, reminding some of the kingly bearing of his grandfather, Vittorio Emanuele II.

Neither was the king, who considered himself a scientist, able to equal the scientific contributions the Duke made on his famous expeditions. In addition, the fact that the Duke and his two brothers were heirs to the throne worried Emanuele until the birth of his son in 1904 assured his own blood line of succession.

In March of 1903, the Duke sailed to New York as a private citizen to receive the prestigious Cullem Medal, awarded for outstanding accomplishment in Arctic discovery by the American Geographical Society. The medal was presented to him by his polar rival, Commander Robert E. Peary, president and founder of the society, who used the occasion to announce the formation of his own North Pole expedition, which would take place in 1905–1906 and attempt to better the Italians' farthest-north record. While in New York, the Duke also promoted his recently completed expedition book, which would be published in English that year as *On the Polar Star in the Arctic*.

When he returned to Italy, the Duke began careful preparations for his next assignment: a diplomatic circumnavigation of the globe, and on August 29, 1903, the *Liguria* disembarked from La Spezia. The Duke would not return to Italy for nineteen and a half months.

The *Liguria's* first stop was New Orleans, where the Duke was asked to settle a dispute among various factions of the Italian community that had been brewing for some time. Next, the vessel docked in Havana, Cuba, where the Duke reported back to Italy about a revolution that had erupted in Santo Domingo in the Dominican Republic.

The Duke wrote that the United States and Germany were equally responsible for destabilizing the government there in order to win influence and take over the tiny republic. His reports also noted that the revolution was due in large part to the extreme poverty of the thousands of jobless peasants who had few other ways to make money than to serve as soldiers for whichever army would pay them.

After stops in Trinidad and Brazil, on New Year's Day, 1904, the *Liguria* sailed into harbor in Buenos Aires, Argentina, where the Italian sailors were warmly received by the city's large Italian population.

From Buenos Aires, the *Liguria* sailed around the tip of South America through the Strait of Magellan to the Pacific, where the Duke visited ports in Chile, Peru, and Mexico, finally arriving in San Francisco. Since Japan and Russia were at war in the North Pacific, the *Liguria* then sailed on into the South Pacific, stopping in the Hawaiian islands, Tahiti, New Zealand, Australia, and China. The Duke also visited Bangkok, where he was hosted by the King of Siam, an acquaintance of the Duke's second eldest brother, who often came to Siam to hunt tiger and elephant.

After calls in Singapore, Java, Madras, Mesewa, and Abyssinia, the *Liguria* sailed back into the familiar waters of the Mediterranean through the Suez Canal, arriving in La Spezia on April 18, 1905. In a circumnavigation lasting 597 days, the ship had covered a total of 53,600 nautical miles, visiting 114 ports and crossing the equator six times.

The Duke and his staff had undertaken extensive scientific observations during the voyage, which resulted in volumes of oceanographic, astronomical, and biological reports. Perhaps the most important aspect of the voyage was that it gave the Duke the idea for his next expedition.

During a visit to Honolulu in May 1904, the Duke had read an obituary for Henry Morton Stanley, the famed English journalist and explorer who had made four expeditions across central Africa. The obituary contained a portion of a speech Stanley had delivered to the Royal Geographical Society in 1901: "I wish that some person devoted to his work, some lover of Alpine climbing, would take the Ruwenzori in hand and make a thorough work of it, explore it from top to bottom, through all those enormous defiles and those deep gorges."

A range of mountains 20 miles (32 kilometers) north of the equator, the Ruwenzori were believed to be the true source of the Nile. Surrounded by as much myth as fact, the range had become legendary as far back as the fifth century B.C., when the Greek tragic poet Aeschylus wrote of "Egypt nurtured by snows that melt into the waters of the Nile." The range was also known as the Mountains of the Moon, from the description of Claudius Ptolemy, an Alexandrian astronomer and geographer of the second century A.D.: "There rises the Mountain of the Moon, whose snows feed the lakes, sources of the Nile."

Over the centuries, ancient Arab mapmakers and members of native caravans had all attested to the existence of a vast group of mountains in central Africa, but had tended to place them in widely divergent locations.

When the first white men arrived in central Africa in the mid-nineteenth century, the existence of these mountains had not yet been confirmed. Indeed, the focus of European exploration was not to find the Ruwenzori but rather the source of the Nile. In 1857, Richard Burton, a thirty-five-year-old diplomat, linguist, and author, was commissioned to locate the source of the Nile. A military officer with the East India Company's Bombay Light Infantry, Burton was accompanied on his quest by Englishman John Hanning Speke. In 1858, after many difficulties, they became the first white men to reach Lake Tanganyika. After Burton was captured by natives, Speke discovered Lake Victoria, which he asserted was the source of the Nile. Burton disputed his claims, even though Speke had undertaken a second expedition in 1862, which led him to the same conclusion. The debate was left unsettled when Speke accidentally shot himself while hunting in 1864.

In 1867, English missionary and explorer David Livingstone set out to resolve the Burton-Speke controversy once and for all, believing that the true headwaters of the Nile lay somewhere beyond Lake Victoria. It was during this expedition that Livingstone disappeared, leading to the famed search organized by the publisher of the *New York Herald Tribune* to find him.[11]

The distinction of being the first explorer to report seeing the Ruwenzori fell to the Italian Romolo Gessi, who apparently glimpsed the range during a circumnavigation of Lake Albert in 1876.

One of the most intrepid explorers ever to venture near the Ruwenzori was Joseph Thompson, a young Scottish geologist who endured three expeditions. On his last journey he was headed northwest from Lake Victoria directly toward the Ruwenzori, but before he was able to record his findings, he was gored by a water buffalo and died.

Not until Stanley's fourth and last expedition in 1888–89 was the existence of the Ruwenzori firmly documented by Europeans. This particular expedition was carried out under contract to King Leopold of Belgium to help establish the Belgian empire all the way from the source of the Nile to the Sudan. In addition, Stanley was also secretly in league with the English in an attempt to relieve a small force of settlers on the upper Nile who were holding off an army of attacking Mahdist rebels from the Sudan. It was during this relief attempt that Mounteney Jephson, a young lieutenant in Stanley's party, saw the snowcapped mountains and became the first person to write down at some length his observations.

Stanley would later claim that in May 1889 he himself first sighted the peaks from the plains near Lake Victoria. When the explorer later wrote of the range, he called it the Ruwenzori, which in the local Mtsora language means "Rainmaker," an appropriate name for this huge massif, which hovers above the perennial mists exhaled by the vast forests, lakes, rivers, and swamps in the equatorial heat. In his characteristic fashion, the explorer re-christened the "huge spiky snow peaks," the Stanley range.

The challenge of Stanley's words—that "some lover of Alpine climbing would take the Ruwenzori in hand and make a thorough work of it"—affected the Duke deeply and inspired him to undertake exploration of the range. By the time the *Liguria* docked at La Spezia, his preliminary plan was formulated. He would attack the mountains at the end of the region's first rainy season in late April or early May (most earlier expeditions had taken place in the fall). This plan gave him less than a year to organize the expedition.

In June 1905, Vittorio Sella was flattered to receive the Duke's invitation to join the expedition as trip photographer and, as on the Mount Saint Elias expedition, to bring along Erminio Botta as his assistant. Umberto Cagni would also be coming, as would Dr. Achille Cavalli Molinelli, who had served as physician on the North Pole expedition, and Dr. Alessandro Roccati, who would collect zoological, botanical, and mineral specimens. Lieutenant Edoardo Winspeare was assigned as the Duke's aide-de-camp.

Also on the expedition roster were Joseph Petigax, the Duke's longtime chief guide, and César Ollier, who, in addition to having climbed with the Duke in the Alps, had guided the Mackinder-Hausberg expedition to Mount Kenya; Joseph Brocherel, who had served on the Mackinder-Hausberg expedition with Ollier; Laurent Petigax, the son of Joseph Petigax; and Gino Gini, the cook who had served on the polar expedition.

Sella's cousin, Filippo De Filippi, who had served as doctor and chronicler for the Mount Saint Elias expedition, declined the Duke's invitation to take part in the Ruwenzori expedition but later wrote up the expedition account from the Duke's notes.

Evidently Stanley's words had also reached the ears of a large number of other explorers. Seven expeditions arrived in the region (on the border between modern-day Uganda and Zaire) within a span of five years, and between 1905 and 1906, four different expeditions made seven attempts on peaks in the Ruwenzori chain. In spite of the number of expeditions to the Ruwenzori, however, none had climbed the tallest summits in the chain, nor had any been able to conduct a systematic and comprehensive scientific study. Most expeditions relied on a few sketchy and worn maps. The Duke hoped to discover new information about the Nile watershed, but the achievement he most wanted was to be the first to reach the Ruwenzori's highest summit.

English explorers Douglas W. Freshfield and Arnold Louis Mumm of the Alpine Club were planning an attempt on the range in the fall of 1906, but when they learned of the Duke's expedition, they hired Moritz Inderbinnen, a famed Swiss guide from Zermatt, and moved their schedule forward an entire year, hoping to steal the prize peaks away from the Italians.

In a letter to Sella, the Duke expressed hope that Freshfield and Mumm would not be able to hire many of the fine climbers already in the region but told Sella to put his plans on hold in case Freshfield succeeded in reaching the highest summit of the Ruwenzori. In that case, the expedition would be called off.

"It's always like that," the Duke wrote to Sella. "For years nobody thought of the Mountains of the Moon—now everybody is rushing to go there."

Freshfield and Mumm set out to make history. They were the first expedition to arrive in the Ruwenzori for the sole purpose of climbing. Reaching the head of the Mobuku Valley in November 1905, they were able to climb to 14,500 feet (4,420 meters)[12] before being driven back by rainstorms and heavy fog. Using out-of-date information and relying on local legend, they had wasted time locating the base of the climb. Even worse, they had tried to climb the mountain during a particularly poor time of year. Distressed, they abandoned the attempt.

When the Duke learned that Freshfield and Mumm had failed, he alerted his colleagues that the Italian expedition to the Ruwenzori was confirmed for the spring of 1906.

From their perch on the rail of the German liner *Burgermeister*, the twelve listless men of the Duke's Ruwenzori expedition watched the barren, sun-baked hills of Africa rise in and out of view. Since departing from Naples on April 16, 1906, they had looked out upon the monotonous horizon of the Red Sea. The boredom of their voyage had so far been broken only by brief visits to the chaotic port bazaars of Said, Suez, Aden, and Djibouti.

The Ruwenzori expedition was not sent off with the fanfare of the Duke's two earlier expeditions. In fact, it had to depart in secret. Just ten days before the *Burgermeister* sailed, Vesuvius—a volcano located just 13 miles (21 kilometers) southeast of Naples—had erupted, sending torrents of lava down the hillsides and burying hundreds of people under a foot of ash and rock. The Duke was aware that for a member of the royal family to leave Italy at a time when there were countless dead, wounded, and homeless would be considered inappropriate. The royal family was expected to visit the region to view the devastation, and many did. The Duke, who could not postpone the expedition, decided to sail, remorseful at being unable to serve his countrymen in their time of need.

As the coast of British East Africa loomed on the horizon, excitement took the place of contrition as the thirty-three-year-old Duke once again felt the thrill of exploration. As a military logistician, the Duke knew that keeping his men safe and well-supplied was of utmost importance. He was aware that previous expeditions to central Africa, including Stanley's, had suffered long periods of privation, that men had starved to death or been weakened by any one of numerous diseases. With his men's safety on his shoulders, no detail was unimportant. Always energetic and sometimes temperamental and impatient, the Duke worked throughout the seventeen-day voyage to Mombasa, either arranging the gear, planning the loads, or taking inventory.

In Mombasa, the Italians transferred their luggage under rain-filled skies to the train that would take them into British East Africa. Unfortunately, Lieutenant Winspeare had become so ill on the voyage that he had to return to Italy on the next ship.

Ahead of them was a two-day, 584-mile (940-kilometer) rail journey to Lake Victoria. In comparison to the dangers faced by the early European explorers, they would be traveling in the lap of luxury. The narrow-gauge railway, the last great engineering feat of the Victorian period, would take them across scorched, waterless desert tangled with thornbush and infested by the lethal tsetse fly.

The British had built the "lunatic line," as it was called in Parliament, to protect the headwaters of the Nile from the colonial interests of Italy. Beginning in 1899, over thirty-two thousand Indian laborers had been imported to construct the railway over a two-year period. More than twenty-five hundred of the workers had been killed by accidents or by lions, who waited near the rail line to attack the men while they worked or drag them out of their tents at night. One pair of lions had managed to kill twenty-eight men before they were caught and killed.

On May 6, 1905, the expedition unloaded at Port Florence on the eastern shores of Lake Victoria and took the steamer *Winifred* to the city of Entebbe.

Because the expedition could not depend upon being able to live off the land or to buy food from local tribes, it had to hire large numbers of porters to carry enough food and gear to survive for months. Food was calculated to last for eighty days—forty days for the trip to and from the Ruwenzori and forty days for the alpine phase of the expedition. The supplies would have to feed an expedition now numbering some three hundred people, including the eleven Italians, almost two hundred porters, the military escort, the caravan leaders, and their servants, as well as those needed to herd the horses, mules, and oxen.

The Duke hired J. Martin, a local tax collector, to organize the caravan and select the carriers. Martin would also escort the expedition to the Ugandan frontier with twenty-seven soldiers and another sixty-seven porters. The expedition was also joined by Signor Bulli, a former member of the Italian Colonial Society, who would help organize provisions for the camp and assist Gino Gini, the cook.

With the work of organizing the people and supplies almost completed, Cagni fell ill and was taken to the hospital on May 8. The Duke was reluctant to leave his close friend behind and put off their departure. However, when Cagni had not improved after three days, the Duke, not wanting to delay the expedition any longer, reluctantly gave the order to move out. Cagni, ever optimistic, suggested from his hospital bed that the Duke leave enough supplies for him to catch up and join the expedition when he recovered. Although he thought Cagni's plea was wishful thinking, the Duke nevertheless left the necessary supplies and wished him well.

The next morning, the Duke was on the path before sunrise, watching the procession of carriers walk past him single-file. By the time the Duke and the nine remaining Italians who were near the end of the caravan started out, the vanguard was well out of sight and on its way to Kampala.

The highland across which the caravan moved alternated between grassland and barren stretches where the brick-red earth was dotted with aca-cia. The open plain was interrupted by dense forest zones in which virgin trees reached more than 100 feet (more than 30 meters) in height. The Italians often took their rest amongst giant shade trees scented heavily with the perfume of acacia, jasmine, and honeysuckle. While monkeys leaped from branch to branch, Sella documented the beauty of equatorial Africa with his camera. The area was known to be afflicted by terrible storms, and the Italians feared that at any moment they might be hit by a sudden cyclone or lightning storm.

The caravan, which usually began as early as 5:30 A.M., marched until the heat of the day, six hours later, covering an average of 14 miles (23 kilometers). Once they had dropped their loads and built their huts, the lively Baganda porters would entertain themselves, the other members of the caravan, and the curious natives who wandered in from nearby villages by wrestling, dancing, and playing musical instruments.

At every stop, a chieftain would come to meet them, bringing a basket full of food, and the Duke, looking slightly bemused, would pose for a photograph. Then there would be a celebration, acccompanied by the sound of trumpets, drums, and horns. Sometimes the band would follow the expedition caravan to the next village. The Italian mountain men soon wearied of these constant rounds of celebration and what the Duke referred to as the "cruelly persistent music."

Despite the noisy interruptions, these friendly ceremonies were an improvement over the tragic encounters that had halted many previous expeditions. Local tribes had been known to ask for tribute before allowing the Europeans to pass, and if the expedition refused to pay, bloodshed often followed.

On May 25, the caravan reached the border of British East Africa, where Martin's escort of soldiers returned to Entebbe. The morning's reveille was no longer sounded by the soldier's trumpets but was replaced by the beating of native drums. Wild game, including elephants, began to appear more frequently. At night, the village music and drumming was succeeded by the roaring of stalking lions just outside the perimeter of the camp.

The anticipated storms now hit the caravan with a vengeance, making the expedition's ascent into the mountains more difficult as the rain turned the paths into a morass of mud through which the porters and the pack animals found it difficult to move.

As the expedition neared Lakes Albert and Albert Edward in the Toro district, the Duke was aware that they were now within sight of the Ruwenzori. The men's eyes scanned the horizon. Twice someone shouted, thinking they had caught sight of the snowy peaks, but they had seen only the white clouds on the horizon.

On May 29, 1906, the expedition was near the place where Jephson had made his initial sighting eighteen years and four days earlier. The Italians remained watchful as they reached a ridge on the hills north of Kaibo, which forms the watershed between Lake Albert Edward and Lake Albert. The Duke halted his men and waited in the quiet and dense fog. Sella set up his photographic equipment, hoping the sky would clear.

Providentially, the clouds parted, and the men gasped in amazement as a gray rock peak covered with snow appeared. With the click of his shutter, Sella became the first photographer to document the existence of the Ruwenzori.

When the expedition arrived in Fort Portal a short time later, they created a stir among the fifteen Europeans in the community. First to greet the Duke were the Reverend A. B. Fisher and his wife, who had twice explored the Mobuku Valley and had gotten as far into the mountains as the Mobuku Glacier.

The Duke also met with Alexander F. R. Wollaston, an acquaintance of his who was there with a British Museum expedition to study the flora and fauna of the Ruwenzori. Wollaston reported that in February he and two other climbers had reached a spur on one of the peaks in the range but were stopped by thick fog at 16,125 feet (4,915 meters). Wollaston and his party had also attempted the Mobuku Glacier in April and reached 16,379 feet (4,992 meters), but the persistently poor weather had turned them back. Wollaston reported that there were still many summits higher than those he had climbed and that it was still unclear which was the best route to follow.

Fearing that someone might have claimed the summits before him, the Duke was quite relieved to hear Wollaston's news and decided to head for the mountains as quickly as possible. If he took the route through the Mobuku Valley, as had all the earlier expeditions, he would find himself blocked by glaciers, deep valleys, and impenetrable ridges. However, if he took another approach, it would mean taking a detour through a region infested with malaria and inhabited by hostile tribes. The Duke decided to take the more direct route up the Mobuku Valley.

On this next leg of the journey steep, muddy mountain paths and difficult crossings through swollen rivers were the major obstacles. The Baganda porters had been cheerful up until this point, but, as they neared the ever-steepening slopes near Bihunga, the last human outpost at 6,300 feet (1,920 meters), they became silent and withdrawn, seeming almost reluctant to continue.

By June 5, the Italians were climbing steep, damp, and slippery slopes through dense forest, thick with leafy undergrowth and rotting trees, and the ascent had degenerated into bushwhacking. Finally, they found just enough solid ground on which to place their seven tents.

The Baganda were people of the plains, and they were now entirely fatigued by the rise in elevation to nearly 8,500 feet (2,591 meters), and the Duke decided to replace them with eighty enthusiastic Bakonjo porters. The Baganda, relieved to be released, left camp in such a hurry that they left behind the food that was owed to them.

Near Nakitawa, the Duke and his guides found a tributary valley not mentioned by previous expeditions. This, the Duke later learned, was the Bujuku Valley, which led to the heart of the chain itself. However, not realizing this at the time, the Duke continued with his plan to follow the route of previous explorers in order to reach a summit from which he could plan his next moves.

The Mobuku Valley was a river of mud, and soon the Italians found themselves sunk up to their knees. To make any progress at all they had to hang onto overhanging branches and pull themselves along. Eventually they reached a plateau covered by a primeval forest. Veils of thick moss hung from every twig, and layers of decaying wood and rotting trunks covered the ground. In this grim, strange, and quiet world no birds flew and no animals came near. The men had to leap from trunk to trunk to avoid falling up to their waists in the mossy bog. Eventually they reached hard ground where violets and other flowers grew along the path. Nearby, a beautiful waterfall flowed, reminding the Italians of their Alps. Although the men wanted to camp here, the Duke was anxious to reach the glacier as soon as possible and gave orders to continue.

Fifty-four days after leaving Naples, the Duke ordered the party to make base camp at 12,461 feet (3,798 meters) under an overhanging ledge at a place called Bujongolo. The site of the base camp was out of the icy winds that blew off the glacier above, but the expedition's tents and sleeping bags were still at a camp farther below. To keep warm, the Italians joined the African porters around a great fire, huddling together under the stars.

When the tents arrived, there was just enough room for six of them. There was little solid ground, just moss and mud, so trees had to be cut to provide planking on which to erect the tents. Waterfalls rained down on either side of the overhanging ledge, and consequently the tents, clothing, and sleeping bags were perpetually wet.

On June 9, Duke set out with Joseph Petigax, César Ollier, Laurent Petigax, Joseph Brocherel, Erminio Botta, and five barefoot Bakonjo porters, now clothed in woolen garments. That same day in Entebbe, the recuperated Cagni began making double marches to join his companions far to the west.

Petigax and Ollier chose a route up a steep, rocky gorge with sheer walls on one side and deep crevasses on the other. Moving quickly and full of excitement, the climbers skirted the crevasses. After two hours of hard climbing they reached the Mobuku Glacier.

The porters' bare feet made the difficult passage up a rock embankment even more dangerous for them, so the Duke sent Botta and Laurent Petigax with them to a camp at the bottom of the glacier. Anxious to push forward, the Duke and the guides continued the climb to the ridge until a thick mist forced them to bivouac on the glacier.

Joseph Petigax, Ollier, Brocherel, and the Duke all had to sleep cramped in a single Whymper tent. Knowing the summit was now within his grasp, the Duke could not sleep or keep his nervousness to himself. It was here at the head of the Mobuku Glacier that Freshfield, Mumm, and their guide Moritz Inderbinnen had been defeated by weather in November 1905.

From 1900 to 1905, only four other parties had explored this far on the glacier above the Mobuku Valley, and all had been defeated by poor weather. Near here the Reverend A. B. Fisher and his wife had been forced to turn back twice.

In January 1906, Herr Grauer, an Austrian mountaineer, with two English missionaries, Maddox and Tegart, had reached the high terminal ridge of the valley at about 15,000 feet (4,572 meters). Thinking he had found the watershed of the mountain chain, Grauer named a small rocky outcropping at 14,813 feet (4,515 meters) King Edward Peak before admitting defeat and retreating.

The thought of failure weighed heavily on the Duke throughout the night. Confined in the cramped tent, waiting for the cold, damp fog to lift, the Duke grew more restless with each passing hour. He knew that his expedition might have to wait days and weeks before the mist lifted. Even then, the rain and snow might continue for weeks.

Throughout their sleepless night, the Italians repeatedly opened the tent flap to check the visibility. On the morning of June 10, the Duke looked out and, to his amazement, saw stars on the horizon. The fog had lifted.

Seized by "an irresistible impatience to proceed" and dreading the return of the fog, the Duke, Petigax, Ollier, and Brocherel hurried to the top of the ridge before daybreak. Quickly, they reached the small rock outcropping that Grauer had named King Edward Peak. From here it was possible to see not just a mountain, but an entire range of mountains stretching before them in every direction.

As the Duke beheld the view, he realized that earlier explorers' perception that the Ruwenzori chain consisted of a group of isolated peaks was incorrect. The entire range was connected by a series of glaciers and ridges.

By 8:00 A.M., they climbed a peak east of the Mobuku Valley, called Semper Peak or Ngemwimbi, which had earlier been attempted by a party of naturalists to a height of 14,900 feet (4,542 meters). The Italians easily ascended the peak to its top at 15,843 feet (4,829 meters), claiming their first virgin summit.

Satisfied with that accomplishment, the Duke led his companions to attack another peak 400 yards along the ridge. Here he became the first to set foot on the highest summit of Kiyanja, a peak named by an English climber called Johnston, who had been forced to give up his try for its summit at about 15,000 feet (4,572 meters).

With the mist already closing in, the Duke ordered the party to retreat. By the time they had found their way to the camp on the Mobuku Glacier, the fog was so thick that they were scarcely able to see their tracks from that morning.

As the Duke and his guides stumbled into camp, they found a second tent beside theirs. Inside were Sella, Laurent Petigax, Botta, and six Bakonjo porters getting ready to climb the next day.

In the morning, however, the fog persisted. Nevertheless, as he had done countless times before, Sella waited patiently with his camera at the ready. Finally, late in the day, the sky cleared, and he was able to photograph the entire Ruwenzori range in a breathtaking sunset.

Sella's view of the Ruwenzori would be the last for nearly a week. Having left the camp on the glacier, the expedition hunkered into their tents at Bujongolo in heavy mist and rain. With little dry wood, they were unable to build fires and kept warm by digging themselves out of the invading mud.

Meanwhile, Cagni, in dawn-to-dusk marches, had been traveling up to 27 miles (44 kilometers) a day, aided by local chiefs. Porters on their way back from the Mobuku Valley with fresh supplies helped him across rivers. With such fortunate assistance, Cagni arrived in Bujongolo on June 16 to find only Doctor Molinelli in camp. The Duke had left with Joseph and Laurent Petigax, Ollier, Brocherel, and Botta to explore the central and highest group of peaks, known as Mount Stanley.

As the party climbed the flanks of the massif, the Bakonjo porters became frightened as they realized they were traveling toward the Congo, which they knew was inhabited by warlike and hostile tribes. Some fled, and the Duke sent the rest back to camp with Botta and Laurent Petigax.

Climbing in dense mist on the early morning of June 18, the Duke, Joseph Petigax, Ollier, and Brocherel were making good progress on hard snow when they came to a ridge. To the south they could see a corniced peak and to the north a rounded snow peak, the two connected by an ice col. The Duke chose to climb the southern peak first, and by 7:30 A.M. all four men had reached the summit. Through the mist they could see that the higher of the two peaks was the northern one, and although it looked possible to climb, the col between the two peaks had dangerous-looking cornices on either side.

Petigax led the men up an ice wall until they were halted by an overhanging cornice. There Petigax, standing with his heavy nailed boots on top of Ollier's shoulders, poked his ice ax through the snow and pulled himself through the hole to the summit. A few minutes later, all four men were standing on the northern peak, at 16,815 feet (5,125 meters) the highest of Mount Stanley's nine peaks.

In the bright sunlight above a sea of clouds, the Duke unfurled the Italian tricolor flag given him by Queen Mother Margherita, with its motto

"*Ardisci e Spera*" ("Dare and Hope"), and planted it on the summit. In honor of his mentor and patron, he named the northern and highest summit Margherita Peak, and in homage to the English explorers who had preceded him on the mountain, he called the 16,749-foot (5,105-meter) southern summit Alexandra Peak after the English queen and wife of King Edward VII.

The Italians had conquered the tallest peaks of the entire Ruwenzori. However, their triumph was short-lived. In the mist they had neglected to wear their sunglasses and now began to suffer from snow blindness. Throughout the night all four men wrestled with their pain, treating their swollen eyes with wet tea leaves, the only remedy they had at hand.

Somewhat recovered the next day, they climbed two more peaks, naming the first, at 16,387 feet (4,995 meters), Elena Peak, in honor of the Italian queen and wife of King Victor Emanuele III, and the second, at 16,338 feet (4,980 meters), Savoia Peak, in honor of the royal house of Savoy.

For the next several weeks, the party climbed in remarkably clear weather, achieving fourteen summits, all above 15,000 feet (4,500 meters). The Duke climbed the four principal peaks of the chain and carried out an array of topographical surveys that confirmed the altitudes of and relationships between the various peaks. The studies also clarified many false assumptions made by earlier explorers—finding, for example, that the Bujuku Valley led directly into the center of the mountain chain.

Most importantly, perhaps, the Italians confirmed that the Ruwenzori chain sheds its waters on all its slopes and in all directions, forming a hydrographic system independent of Lake Victoria. The waters from six separate mountain ranges in the Ruwenzori feed into the same river basin, forming the southwest source of the Nile. The Duke's studies determined that the true source of the Nile lay somewhere in the Congo, a short distance to the west of the Semliki Valley.

At one point, the Duke had the joy of seeing all his men spread out in various projects across the entire mountain chain. Sella and his caravan were working their way up the summit of Alexandra Peak to photograph. Cagni was measuring altitudes and taking magnetic observations, while Roccati was making geological surveys and Molinelli was collecting flora and fauna. Through an opening in the fog the Duke could also see the fires of the Bakonjo porters, who were bringing up supplies from the villages far below.

Unlike many of the earlier explorers of the area, the Duke chose not to substitute European names for the native names of lakes, glaciers, and peaks, christening only unnamed peaks that he and his party had climbed or mapped. Mostly he named peaks after members of his family. He did not give his own name to any of the summits, but later he was "forced" to yield to a proposal by the Royal Geographical Society that the peak he had called Mount Thompson be renamed Mount Luigi di Savoia.

Cagni had recuperated sufficiently from his illness to climb three peaks, one of which bears his name. Sella, with Botta, climbed and photographed spectacular views from nine peaks, including Mobius Peak, the last of Mount Stanley's unclimbed peaks. Sella also climbed the central peak of Mount Luigi di Savoia, a peak that now bears his name.

Before leaving the Ruwenzori for good, the Duke took Sella and Botta, his guides, and seventeen Bakonjo porters to explore the Bujuku Valley. On their way out they made the first ascent of a peak the Duke named Mount Gessi (15,470 ft/4,715 m) in honor of Romolo Gessi, the Italian explorer who had first circumnavigated Lake Albert and reported seeing the Ruwenzori. Mount Gessi is separate from the principal range, and from its summit it is possible to see the other five principal groups of the Ruwenzori all in a line. Taking advantage of the unusual clarity of the air, the Duke took a panoramic view of the conquered summits. Alone, he remained a long time on the summit of this, his sixteenth first ascent, slowly savoring the exultation of his accomplishment.

In Italy, the Duke resumed a simple life. He arose early each day and worked on the Ruwenzori expedition account from nine until one o'clock. He then wrote letters or worked on the expedition photographs with Sella until late afternoon, when he took a two-hour bicycle ride. After dinner, he worked to midnight.

On January 1, 1907, the Duke gave the first of many lectures on the expedition—this one before the entire court, including King Emanuele, Queen Elena, and Queen Mother Margherita.

On January 7, he gave a lengthy report of the expedition before the Italian Geographic Society in Rome, with Sella providing limelight lantern slides he had developed for the speaking tour.

On January 14, 1907, the Duke appeared before the Royal Geographical Society in London. Stanley's appearance at the Royal Albert Hall in 1890 had drawn thousands. The Duke's lecture was a much smaller affair, held in Queen's Hall of Buckingham Palace. For the first time in the history of the Royal Geographical Society, however, the King of England was host for the meeting.

Decorated palms and a large array of plants were placed around the room to simulate the "Dark Continent," and twenty-two hundred significant guests attended, including members of the royal family, Britain's most powerful politicians, all the ranking international diplomats, and Britain's senior military staff, including the Himalayan explorer Sir Martin Conway. They had all come to see the Italian explorer who had answered Stanley's call. Wearing elegant formal wear, the thirty-four-year-old olive-skinned Duke appeared younger, healthier, and more polished than the hardy adventurer the guests had expected.

Speaking in perfect "scholarly English," the Duke recounted, not without emotion, the story of the expedition in full detail. The audience was entranced by Sella's breathtaking photographs, and at the end of the evening the king was profuse in his praise.

In the following months the Duke continued to receive honors from his peers. Edward Whymper wrote that Mount Saint Elias and the Ruwenzori could have been climbed by less skillful mountaineers, but what was to be admired in the Duke's expeditions were "the perfect management, the adoption of the right means to attain the ends, and the completeness of the manner in which the results were attained."

To some, Whymper continued, the Duke's Ruwenzori account would most certainly "yield more attractive reading" and gain even wider acceptance had it met with "accidents and horrors" as earlier expeditions had. But to Whymper, the absence of such dramatic events was proof of the preparation, time, and trouble taken to prevent them.

By 1907, in every European and American capital, newspaper editors were asking their countrymen why they could not produce someone as accomplished as the young Duke of the Abruzzi, who in less than ten years had beaten the most expert climbers and explorers in the world on the mountains of Alaska, on the ice of the North Pole, and in the heart of Africa.

Chapter Six

❦

The Duke and
His American Princess

In December 1907, the Duke made diplomatic visits to Ireland and Scotland on his new battleship, the *Regina Elena*. In Glasgow, he presented his Ruwenzori address to the Scottish Royal Geographical Society. Once again, King Edward VII was in the audience, having canceled his social engagements to travel to Glasgow to meet his young friend.

During the lecture, the Duke was asked when he would take on the challenge of the "Third Pole"—an altitude record in the Himalaya. Few in the audience were aware that the Duke was already using his influence with King Edward to obtain permission to climb in the British Punjab. The Duke took the occasion to announce that the Third Pole would indeed be his next objective, but not until the following year or two. Until then he was committed to a demanding schedule of naval duties, diplomatic functions, and patriotic events.

When he found time for pleasure, the Duke often chose to live as an ordinary private citizen. He occasionally traveled alone in larger cities, walking incognito through busy places full of people. Stories about his unexpected wanderings sometimes reached the newspapers and were reminiscent of his father's strolls through the streets of Madrid during his brief reign as king of Spain.

The Duke preferred eating alone at a restaurant in Rome or Turin to being accompanied by an entourage. Driving alone to his favorite spa at the

Italian resort of Salsomaggiore, he would dine unrecognized among the other guests and afterwards join in card games, pantomimes, or lively debates. His very modesty and simplicity were his best disguise. Even in the alpine resorts where he went to climb, his demeanor was so inconspicuous that no one recognized him as the explorer who had challenged Peary in the race to the Pole and fulfilled Stanley's wish in the Ruwenzori.

What the Duke could not disguise, however, was the interest he created among women the moment he entered a room. An acquaintance of his noted that the Duke, in turn, made every effort to return their admiring gazes. He often spent the evening in the company of several women without giving away his real intentions or identity, thus earning the reputation of being a "taciturn flirt." But these private occasions were rare. Most of his time was spent in the public eye.

The crowned heads of Europe looked upon the Duke as Italy's finest and most available bachelor of royal blood. Both Kaiser Wilhelm II of Germany and his uncle, King Edward VII, admired the Duke for his mountaineering and yachting achievements. The Kaiser was keen to have the Duke marry a German princess to cement Italy's membership in the Triple Alliance. King Edward wanted him to marry an English princess. In the end, both were disappointed. The Duke, while an ardent admirer of women, seemed immune to the attentions of the royal princesses paraded before him. Having circled the globe several times and visited every continent, he was truly a man of the world, influenced by many cultures, particularly by America, where people could marry outside their class.

As a prince of the ruling family, however, the Duke was expected to marry with political considerations in mind, even though he was well down the line of succession to the Italian throne, and a royal marriage would mean little to him in practical terms. The assumption was that should he be unhappy with his spouse, he could always take the path of his uncle Umberto, who had maintained three separate residences to accommodate his two mistresses in addition to Queen Margherita. The Duke found this idea distressing and often confided to close associates that he felt royal marriage was a limited and sheltered existence akin to slavery.

Indeed, Luigi Amedeo had shown signs at an early age that he would follow his heart instead of the dictates of tradition. There's a popular but undocumented story that tells how at ten years old, while strolling in the country outside Turin with his two nurses, the young prince met a gypsy who attempted to tell his fortune.

"You will one day sit on the throne, and your papa will get you the most beautiful queen in the world," the gypsy had told him.

"Fuoco di Sant'Antonio ('Fire of Saint Anthony')!" the boy is said to have replied. "A lot you know! I shall be a sailor, and I shall travel all over the world and marry whom I please!"

In the years that followed, the Duke's attitude toward matrimonial matters changed little. As he grew into manhood, his marriage was a frequent topic of discussion between King Umberto and Queen Margherita, as they attempted to find him a wife.

When the Duke returned from the Mount Saint Elias expedition, the king had been anxious to capitalize on Luigi Amedeo's popularity by arranging a royal wedding. The Duke, however, begged off for the time being, pleading that he needed to give all his attention to his upcoming North Pole expedition. King Umberto's assassination while the Duke was away at the Pole further postponed the question, and the Duke was greatly relieved that he had not had to confront "that horrible marriage."

The Duke was a deeply private man, who rarely discussed his personal life even with his closest companions, and had it not been for a chance encounter with a young American woman, he no doubt would have succeeded in keeping his romantic interests to himself.

According to the British newspapers of the day, the Duke met Katherine Elkins in the late summer of 1906 at a party held in his honor at Lake Como, where he often went to relax after his expeditions or alpine climbs. Katherine was visiting from Rome, where her parents (her father was a wealthy businessman and politician) rented a villa each summer while they sought out Italian antiques and fine Italian marble to furnish the family home in West Virginia.

The Duke was immediately struck by this beautiful auburn-haired woman with a piercing gaze and a glint of willful daring in her eyes. Forthright and well educated, Katherine was also well versed in the social graces. Apparently, the attraction was mutual. Their affair would capture the hearts of the world and become the most publicized romance of the age.

Other reports say that the Duke and Katherine met early in the spring of 1907 in Washington, D.C., when the Duke was sent as King Vittorio

Emanuele III's official representative to America's tercentenary exposition in Jamestown, Virginia. The exact circumstances of their meeting are in some dispute. The *Corriere della Sera* in Milan wrote that the Duke first met Katherine at a private party held by the former secretary of the American ambassador to Rome, while the *New York Times* reported that the couple met at a party held by a naval attaché. Both newspapers agreed, however, that from the moment of their first meeting Katherine and the Duke were constantly in each other's company.

And so began the rumors. One newspaper wrote that Katherine had been expected to attend a party held at the Italian Embassy but had gone riding on her new horse instead and had forgotten all about the Duke, who supposedly had been so charmed by the incident that he had immediately proposed. When questioned as to whether the Duke had proposed, she flatly dismissed the speculation.

Some suggested that Miss Elkins already had everything a princess could want and would not marry the Duke. Katherine remained noncommittal, telling reporters that she would marry the Duke "if he were an American."

The prospect of an American debutante being courted by an Italian prince was hardly unusual. Many rich American women had abandoned their homeland and families for the prestige of a royal title in Europe. Nor was this the first time the newspapers had gossiped about Katherine, whose numerous romances were well documented. The most interesting part of the story was that Katherine was considered by the press to be the most unconventional girl in Washington.

Affable and energetic, Katherine rode her expensive horses well in the hunt and drove her touring car at high speeds through the streets of late-night Washington. She had been courted by some of society's richest young men. It was said that she had the fortunate faculty of making herself agreeable to princes as well as to bounders and was often found in the company of both.

When the thirty-four-year-old Duke arrived in Washington in 1907, Katherine was a twenty-one-year old American princess. Her father, Stephen Benton Elkins, represented West Virginia in the U.S. Senate. Her mother, Hallie, the senator's second wife, was herself the daughter of another influential senator, Henry Gassaway Davis.

Davis had mentored the young Elkins to prominence in Washington politics and had arranged for the promising senator to marry his daughter, whereupon the two men had become wealthy and successful business partners, with interests in coal mines, timber, and railroads. Elkins's successful speculation in numerous land holdings across the western states made him at one point the largest single landowner in America. With their riches, Davis and Elkins had built an entire modern town that they called Elkins, located about 150 miles (241 kilometers) due west of Washington in West Virginia.

The Elkinses possessed numerous homes—in Washington, D.C., in New York, and in West Virginia, where the senator had built an eighteen-thousand-square-foot, thirty-one-room mansion that he named Halliehurst after Katherine's mother. With its turrets and porticoes the exterior of Halliehurst resembled a European castle. Its vast gardens were decorated with Italian marble statuary and tended by Italian workers hired by Senator Elkins on his trips to Italy. The interior featured modern appliances, including central heating and electricity, as well as telephones and a prototype of Marconi's wireless machine.

Katherine spent most of her time at Halliehurst, where she lived quietly with her mother and four older brothers. However, when she came to Washington, Katherine's life was that of a spirited and modern city girl. One night during the Duke's visit to Washington, Katherine promised him an evening he would not forget and gave him his choice: dinner, a dance, or an evening at the theater. Already royally smitten, the Duke replied, "I'll take all three."

The Duke's stay in Washington, D.C. ended when King Vittorio Emanuele III sent him on a diplomatic mission to the Italian community in New York, with the intention of influencing the thousands of Italian immigrants who had become U.S. citizens to vote for policies favorable to Italy.

At 7:00 A.M. on May 25, 1907, as the warship *Varese* entered New York harbor under his command, the Duke gave orders to fire a thirteen-gun salute to the U.S. colors. From Fort Wadsworth, the Americans returned a twenty-one-gun salute. As the ship dropped anchor at the West 79th Street pier, thousands of Italians wearing their best Sunday clothes—black derby hats, wing-collar shirts, and black ties for the men; traditional garments for the women—waved the tricolor flag of Italy from buildings and streets along the shoreline. However, while everyone was trying to catch sight of the Duke, he was already on his way to a vigorous round of official visits led by Count Massiglia, the Italian consul general. In one day he attended an opera, ate in an Italian restaurant, met with the mayor, dedicated an Italian statue, and made several speeches to various Italian organizations.

During his stay in New York, the Duke was invited to be the special guest of honor at a meeting of the American Alpine Club in the grand ballroom of the Hotel Astor. The *New York Times* reported that the ballroom was decorated with Jacquemincot roses mixed with alpine edelweiss. Great blocks of ice were carved into mountains with tiny ice climbers roped together on the peaks.

The occasion honored a number of alpinists and explorers, including Arctic explorer David L. Brainerd of the Greely polar expedition and Annie S. Peck, who had climbed to 20,500 feet (6,248 meters) on Bolivia's Mount Sorata in the northern section of the Cordillera Real. Also in attendance was the Duke's good friend Professor Charles Fay, who had founded the club in 1902 and was then serving as its first president.

The other notable guest on the dais that evening was Commander Robert Edwin Peary, who conferred upon the Duke an honorary membership in the American Alpine Club. As in 1903, when he had used the occasion of presenting the Duke with the Cullem Medal for Arctic exploration to announce his own upcoming North Pole expedition, Peary again took advantage of the large audience of explorers to announce that his 1905–1906 expedition had beaten the Duke's farthest-north record. Whether Peary had indeed succeeded in doing what he claimed is a matter of debate among present-day polar historians.

Taking 29 men, 120 dogs, and 50 Eskimo drivers and laborers, Peary had traveled to north Grant Land and then west to Cape Hecla, reportedly getting as far as 87°6' north latitude, some 36 miles (58 kilometers) closer to the Pole than the Italian record. What created the controversy was Peary's phenomenal pace between April 14 and April 21, 1906. By his own measurements, he had traveled 130 miles (209 kilometers) due north at an average speed of 19 miles (31 kilometers) per day over drifting pack ice and without experienced men to break trail, as Petigax had done for Cagni. Neither Nansen nor Cagni had averaged more than 7 miles (11 kilometers) per day. Peary's "beeline" has been questioned over the years by researchers who doubted his ability to cross vast expanses of ice in a straight line toward the Pole when other explorers, like the Italians and Norwegians, had seldom found any long stretches of smooth ice.

In addition to his astonishing speed record, Peary also claimed to have discovered some islands that he named Crocker Land, after a prominent financier of the Peary Arctic Club. It took researchers until 1914 to learn that Crocker Land did not even exist.

Finally, unlike other Arctic explorers, Peary did not keep a journal and never recorded detours, backtracking, or problems such as bad weather, open sea, or large hummocks. Wally Herbert, an English polar explorer and historian, suggests that Peary may have beaten the Italian record, but not by much more than a mile. However, by not keeping accurate records, Peary was in the end unable to prove that he had truly beaten Cagni's farthest-north record.

Despite the honors and interest accorded the Duke for his explorations, American newspapers were far more interested in reporting on his love life. Once, in Washington, the Duke and Katherine had been caught off guard by reporters on their way to a formal military event. The next day, the papers carried the story that during a sudden downpour, the Duke had gallantly covered Katherine with his jacket and then carried her over a muddy path to a corner grocery store, where they embraced under an awning. Some papers reported that the Duke had proposed and been rejected, others that he had proposed and been accepted. Even when the Duke returned to Italy, the stories continued to proliferate.

American reporters kept a vigil near the Elkins estate in West Virginia, waiting for Katherine to ride her horse into town twice a day to pick up her mail. It was said the Duke was also sending her love notes from his warship via the new Marconi wireless.

Even the most cynical aristocrats and society columnists on both sides of the Atlantic finally succumbed to the allure of the Duke and Katherine's fairytale romance. But their blissful beginning was about to become far more complicated.

In February 1908, several Italian reporters went to La Spezia to seek confirmation of the Duke's rumored engagement to the last unwed English princess, Patricia of Connaught. To their surprise, the Duke was not aboard the *Regina Elena*. They searched for him on land but could not find him. He was not in Turin, in Paris, or even in England. Unbeknownst to everyone, the Duke was sailing to Cuba under the false name of Luigi Sarto.

From Havana the Duke continued on to Florida, where Katherine was waiting with her mother at Palm Beach. Traveling in secret in Katherine's auto, they crossed five states, finally arriving in Washington, D.C., where a crowd of American and European journalists awaited them. The clandestine nature of the Duke's visit to America was seen as an admission of the couple's pending engagement, and on March 18, 1908, half-page photographs of Katherine and the Duke appeared in the *New York Times*, which virtually announced their forthcoming marriage.

Since reporters were watching every train station in Washington, Katherine drove the Duke to Baltimore, where he boarded a train to New York, still traveling under the assumed name of Sarto. Before he could embark for Italy aboard the *Lusitania*, the reporters caught up with him on board the ship. Stationing themselves in the corridor outside his cabin, they besieged him the entire night until the Duke lost patience and shouted at them, in English, that he had no intention of being interviewed and to leave him in peace!

Arriving in London on March 26, the Duke, wearing a derby hat and neat gray suit, posed jokingly with a mob of reporters as he disembarked. Asked if he was successful in proposing to Katherine, he answered, "I don't look disappointed do I?"

In Italy, the story of the Duke's romance aroused more surprise than interest. The most surprised and concerned were the members of the royal House of Savoy. Jealous of their privacy, they now saw themselves the subject of daily press coverage, which speculated about their traditions, secrets, and history.

Put into a very public position about the affair, the press-shy King Vittorio Emanuele III could neither confirm nor deny the marriage proposal of his cousin. His vague replies were interpreted as opposition to the marriage, and the press began to write of the king's long-standing jealousy toward the Duke, postulating that he was now exacting his revenge by not letting the Duke marry Katherine.

A *New York Times* story pictured the Duke as a brave explorer who would not be "frozen out of his love affair by his royal cousin's frigidity, nor shrink from the obstacles the king may throw in his way." The unkindest cut came from the Italian press, which quoted an unnamed friend of the Duke as saying that the king himself had "married a descendant of a Montenegrin shepherd . . . from a semi-civilized court."

Ironically, Queen Elena was quite fond of the Duke. Though having no influence over her husband, she often assured the Duke that she would gladly accept Katherine Elkins.

The king offered the press only an ambiguous announcement that said little to clarify his position: "Luigi, my dearest cousin, is an honor to the present generation," he said. "I can deny him nothing."

The Duke immediately retreated from public view to work on the publication of his Ruwenzori book. His private life was virtually gone, and the days when he could wander unnoticed in public were over. His photographs were constantly seen in newspapers and magazines. Everything he once did spontaneously now had to be done under the scrutiny of the press. As one newspaper story quipped, he was "like a criminal out on bail."

From his battleship in port at La Spezia, the Duke spent much of his time seeking his family's permission to marry Katherine Elkins. He corresponded frequently with his eldest brother, Emanuele Filiberto, the Duke of Aosta, who, however, was the first to publicly oppose Luigi di Savoia's marriage to Katherine.

Emanuele Filiberto was four years older than the Duke and had been trained in the military. He was as athletic and handsome as his brother Luigi Amedeo, but in matters of love he was quite different.

Emanuele Filiberto had made no compromises in love. He had wed for political reasons when he had taken the beautiful Hélène of Orléans, a member of the noble French house of Bourbon, as his wife. Affectionately called "the Princess of France," Hélène was described as possessing a piety that was "strong and deep." She not only represented the Savoy family well at home and abroad but had produced two male heirs. In public, she, like her husband, was not in favor of the Duke's marriage to a foreign commoner.

The Duke's second eldest brother, the thirty-eight-year-old Vittorio Emanuele, Count of Turin, was the only one in the family who spoke up for Luigi's marriage. "Let him do what he likes," he said to reporters. "Why interfere?"

The press was never far away when the three Aosta brothers met to discuss the Duke's marriage. Emanuele Filiberto must have reminded Luigi that that it would be unthinkable to marry outside his rank. And he and others of his family no doubt insisted that if they did marry their marriage would be morganatic—Katherine would remain untitled and their children would not inherit the Duke's title or the Savoy fortune.

Failing to enlist the support of the king or his eldest brother, the Duke turned to Queen Margherita at her court in Rome. However, in public announcements the Queen Mother gave only lukewarm approval of her nephew's marriage, commenting simply that she had seen enough American ladies to "appreciate their merits as women and wives."

Lacking the support of his family, the Duke took solace in the kind words of his friends. Early in April, Vittorio Sella wrote the Duke to add his encouragement to the marriage: "Now that the news is confirmed by those newspapers in which I have confidence, let me say that Your Highness has acted in my opinion with logic and good sense in contracting marriage with a young American lady of rare perfection. To these sincere impressions of mine, I take the liberty of adding the most cordial congratulations from myself and my wife, with the most vivid wish that your Royal Highness find true and desired happiness."

In the midst of trying to secure his family's consent to his marriage, the Duke was called to duty on April 18, 1908, to command a vessel in Turkish waters off the coast of Libya as part of a military response to the murder of a Catholic priest in Tripoli. The assignment was a prestigious one for the Duke, who was expected to be named admiral on the king's birthday, November 11, 1908. The Italian newspapers speculated that the betrothal of Katherine to the Duke would also be announced at the same time—the king's birthday being the traditional occasion when such family news would be made public.

While the Duke was away at sea, support for his marriage came from an unlikely source. The people of Albania[13] were already calling "Catarina" their queen and wanted the Duke to be their first king. If he were a king himself, the Duke would be free to marry Katherine without his cousin's approval.

In America, speculation about the marriage of Katherine and the Duke ran from the simply humorous to the grotesque. Someone traced the Elkins family tree forty-two generations back to Charlemagne, and it was suggested

13 *The Duke (center) with guides Joseph Petigax and César Ollier stopping in the forest during the Ruwenzori expedition*

14 Mount Stanley, the highest group of peaks in the Ruwenzori

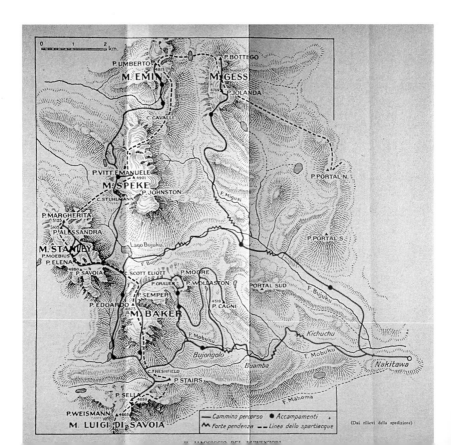

16 Katherine Elkins

17 *Halliehurst, the Elkins home in West Virginia*

18 *The Duke at age forty*

19 *The Duke's party crossing the Baltoro Glacier during the K2 expedition*

21 Camp XII prior to the attempt on Bride Peak (Chogolisa)

22 Route of the K-2 expedition

≺ *20 K2 from the southern side of Staircase Peak*

23 *Icefall on the Baltoro with Mustagh Tower in the background*

that Senator Elkins, by virtue of the Duke's marriage to his daughter, would attain the right of succession—however remote—to the Italian throne. Referring to his multi-million-dollar business empire and his vast land holdings in West Virginia, Senator Elkins commented: "Why should I desire another title seeing that I am already prince of Princeton, king of Kingwood, and monarch of Morgantown?"

Perhaps no one demonstrated less outward concern about the pending marriage than Katherine herself. It was evident to many of her friends that while she was shopping for wedding garments, she was also growing weary of the numerous cables and telegrams the Duke was sending from Italy. Her closest friends suggested that the high-spirited Katherine would never consent to live in a place where she was not welcome, especially one so far away from her family.

There were endless proposals and counterproposals to consider. Katherine would have to convert to Catholicism and receive the Pope's blessing to live with the Duke in Italy. However, obtaining the Pope's approval would not be easy. Years before Pius IX had excommunicated King Vittorio Emanuele II, the Duke's grandfather and head of the Savoy family, when the king had annexed the papal states in forming the new Italy, and papal hostility to the Savoys still lingered.

As a forthright American Katherine had little understanding of and less patience with these subtleties and was convinced that King Vittorio Emanuele III, if he wanted to, had the authority to resolve all the complications. No doubt her unspoken hope was that the Duke would take a firm position and confront the king.

Katherine's father was beginning to doubt that the Duke would ever take a stand against his family. While there was no question as to the Duke's physical bravery, as witnessed by his expeditions, Senator Elkins nevertheless felt that the Duke did not have the strength of character required to marry his daughter. On October 16, 1908, the senator gave an interview on the porch of his home in Washington, D.C., in which he made derogatory remarks about royalty in general, and about the Duke in particular. "Seeing that the Duke does not want to come to this country and work like any other American gentleman," he said, "I would prefer that my daughter marry a Randolph County schoolmaster."

The senator's remarks were carried widely by the press at the same time as stories that the Duke would be made King of Albania and that Katherine would become Queen Catarina. Ironically, the senator's remarks caused many American editors to defend the Duke.

"How far would the job of King of Albania have to go to satisfy the senator's idea of working like an American gentleman?" asked the *New York Times* in an editorial. "It seems to us that few American gentlemen would have harder work than a king in Albania." Some editors suggested that since the Duke was also about to become an admiral, perhaps the senator had a poor opinion of a naval commander's job as well.

The senator's remarks were a strong blow for the Duke. He did not have the approval of his family, and now Katherine's father was also against him.

After conferring with his brother Emanuele Filiberto at his palace in Capodimonte near Naples, a downcast and tired Duke visited Queen Margherita's chateau in Stupingi. Those in court who had witnessed the Duke pleading his case before King Vittorio Emanuele III on previous occasions knew that Luigi di Savoia had little chance of persuading the king or the rest of his family. One person at court described a typical meeting between the Duke and his family: "The king never contradicts the Duke nor never shows any sign of displeasure, the Queen smiles warmly, and Queen Margherita is cool to the Duke, who does all the talking."

After visiting Margherita, the Duke once again disappeared. Numerous searches failed to locate him, and it was rumored that he was meeting Katherine somewhere in Europe. On October 25, however, the Duke reappeared in Rome, where he was due to promote the publication of his Ruwenzori book. Asked about his whereabouts, the Duke answered only that he no longer wanted to be a prince.

An editorial in the *New York Times* the next day said: "There are plenty of princes, but if he writes a book, does daring deeds, or betroths himself to a rich man's daughter, the size of his shoes will become the subject of public comment."

On Sunday, November 1, the *New York Times* published a large photograph of Katherine Elkins elegantly clothed in the latest style on the front page of the paper's feature section. On several occasions a photograph of her had appeared in East Coast newspapers, but the *Times* rarely went to such extravagance for a story.

The article inside stated that the engagement of Katherine and the Duke of the Abruzzi was expected to be announced on November 11, the birthday of King Vittorio Emanuele III. That same day, the story reported, the Duke was to be named rear admiral. However, the long-anticipated day came and went without an announcement from the king. On Sunday, November 15, the *New York Times* carried another full-page story and photos devoted to Katherine and her life at Halliehurst, while on an adjoining page was a lavish review of the Duke's Ruwenzori book. Still no wedding announcement was forthcoming from Rome.

On Monday morning, Senator Elkins stepped out of his Washington home to meet with the press, who waited in hushed anticipation of a marriage announcement. Reading from a prepared text the senator stated, "My daughter and the Duke of the Abruzzi are not engaged to be married." A wave of confusion spread through the throng of journalists, who thought they must have misheard him. In his booming voice, the senator continued: "I regret exceedingly the annoyance that must come to the Duke and his family." Responding to a question from reporters, the senator stated simply that he did not know the Duke well outside of the success of his explorations, then turned and went inside, leaving the reporters with their mouths agape.

The next day, a story appeared in newspapers up and down the East Coast—not about the end of the affair, but about the senator's attempt to stop the affair. A reporter had found out that Senator Elkins had asked the town postmaster in Elkins, West Virginia, to seize all of Katherine's mail. The postmaster admitted to returning a package containing a ruby ring to the sender, the Duke of the Abruzzi, who had repackaged it in a plain envelope and sent it again. This time, the postmaster, at the senator's request, sent the envelope to the federal customs officials in Pittsburgh, Pennsylvania, who presented the Duke with a tax of $3,000 on the ring, which was valued at approximately $5,000.

The newspaper article created a scandal. After surviving decades of political infighting to become a respected legislator with a remarkable record of achievement, Elkins was not able to recover from the story of the opened letter. His public image was destroyed; he was now the scoundrel who had destroyed the love affair between his daughter and the Duke of the Abruzzi. Until his part in the affair of the ring had been made public, Elkins had been a leading candidate for the Republican nomination for president. Now his ambitions for greater power were at least temporarily dashed.

At the year's end, the Duke sent a prepared statement to the press, his first and only words on the affair. "I would have been the happiest of husbands if I could have arrived at an agreement with the head of the Elkins family on certain formalities of the marriage ceremony and on some other points, but the Elkinses are so fierce and proud!" he wrote. "I would be very unlucky if I knew not that generally Americans keep their word at any price, because only Katherine, who has promised to devote her life to my happiness, can compensate for the sorrow I have suffered, on one side from my relatives' opposition and on the other side from the rude, insolent, and contemptible vulgarity of the American newspapers."

In Italy, there were different interpretations of the breakup of the engagement, with the blame focusing on King Vittorio Emanuele III and his jealousy of the Duke. People questioned why the Duke did not rebel against the king and marry Katherine in spite of the opposition of the Savoy family. In answer, it was said that the Duke was not a rich man and that he could not afford to lose the privileges of his rank and his stipend from the Royal Navy. His marriage against the will of the king would have automatically robbed him of his official position.

However, it was not true that the Duke did not have his own means. The Aosta family had properties and income from their father's inheritance as well as from their mother's family fortune. But it was not just the lack of money that stopped him from marriage. It is certain that leaving Italy and his naval career would have been very painful for Luigi di Savoia. If he had come to America, his pride would have suffered from the slander that he was taking advantage of Katherine's large dowry. However, all these conjectures are not convincing arguments.

In his recent book, *Il Duca degli Abruzzi*, Italian journalist Gigi Speroni suggests that that the real reason for the marriage breakup was the revelation in newspaper scandal sheets of Senator Elkins's supposed involvement in illegal contracts and special concessions for his railway business.

According to the American weekly *Cosmopolitan*, Senator Elkins and his partners had tried to amend existing laws in order to appropriate $10 million a year in revenues from the West Virginia state treasury. Senator Elkins had also been accused of diverting public funds and using his influence to halt public investigations concerning illegal contracts for his mining concessions in New Mexico.

Although Elkins was never formally charged or brought to trial, Speroni postulates that it is probable that King Vittorio Emanuele III was informed of these accusations by the Italian ambassador and did not want his family linked with a person whose reputation was tainted with such heavy suspicions. If the king had given the Duke these reasons for opposing the marriage, it is understandable that a person of such strict principles as Luigi di Savoia would have accepted the decision without protest.

Washington society circulated its own story, according to which Katherine had married as an adolescent, against the wishes of her family. She had later divorced, but the Duke, a devout Catholic, would not have been able to marry a divorced woman without an annulment of the preceding marriage by the Vatican, which he was not able to obtain.

Luigi di Savoia would have other loves but would never marry. Katherine married in 1913—and later divorced—but continued to wear a diamond and emerald ring the Duke had given her, as well as a medallion containing a lock of his hair. The walls of her room were covered with his photographs, and in her will, she stipulated that she be buried with a bracelet that had been another gift from the Duke. When she died in 1936, three years after the Duke, at the age of fifty, her funeral was delayed until at last the bracelet was found and placed upon her wrist.

Chapter Seven

❦

K2
The Third Pole

AS THE DUKE'S TUMULTUOUS YEAR OF 1908 DREW TO A CLOSE, REPORTERS wrote about his "grieving in seclusion" over the loss of Katherine and that he was ready to resign from the navy because he had not been named admiral as expected in November.

When the story was published, several naval officers sent a petition to Queen Elena pleading against the Duke's resignation. Because the young officers had stepped outside regular channels of authority, the Ministry of the Navy had them arrested. They were later released following a public outcry.

This embarrassing episode caused the Duke to retreat even further from the public eye until, on December 28, 1908, an earthquake struck southern Calabria and eastern Sicily. The towns of Reggio and Messina were devastated, and more than 150,000 people were killed by collapsing buildings and a huge tidal wave. The Duke was placed in command of several ships bringing much-needed supplies to the survivors.

During the relief operations, the Duke's old friend and aide, Umberto Cagni, presumably acting under the orders of the Duke, caused an international incident that once again placed Luigi di Savoia in the center of controversy.

Timber was badly needed to fortify the buildings destroyed by the earthquake. According to a British newspaper story, Cagni discovered that an English ship carrying timber was nearby and demanded that the captain turn over the lumber. When the captain refused, Cagni said he would sink the vessel. The captain informed Cagni that the timber belonged to the English and that he had the might of England behind him. To this Cagni supposedly replied, "First, the timber, then I will deal with England."

Fortunately, England held no grudge against the Duke over Cagni's impulsive act, and early in 1909 he received permission from the British to climb K2 and explore the Baltoro Glacier in the British Punjab. His intention was to establish a new altitude record among the highest mountains in the world, and he immediately wrote to his colleagues to tell them the news.

On January 6, Vittorio Sella received a letter from the Duke marked "Confidential," inviting him to participate in the expedition. The Duke wrote that he was thinking of selecting a small group consisting of four or five climbers and seven or eight Val d'Aosta guides and porters.

"Do you wish to be the photographer?" the Duke asked. "Are you still inclined or have you had enough of expeditions and of my temper, which is not so easy during these trips?"

It was the first time the Duke had so openly acknowledged his temper, but even so, Sella was not enthusiastic about the invitation. Sella's career as an enterprising mountain photographer had begun to take shape in 1890, when he made his first large sale of 130 prints from his Caucasus expedition to the Royal Geographical Society. That same year in America, Professor Charles Fay had introduced Sella's photos to the Appalachian Mountain Club of Boston. They were so well received that in 1893 Fay organized a much larger series of exhibitions. More than twenty thousand visitors came to see Sella's photographs in various galleries, including those of the American Geographical Society, the Museum of Natural History in New York, and the Boston Art Club.

Sella's popularity had been secured in Italy when he photographed Queen Margherita's climb to Punta Gnifetti on Monte Rosa to inaugurate the summit house in 1893. An exhibit of more than four hundred of his mountain photos were later exhibited in Turin to widespread acclaim. By 1909, the fifty-year-old photographer had earned wide respect in Italy, England, and America. His photographs were often sold at prices usually reserved for paintings, and with more success on the horizon, he did not want to leave his work for a six-month expedition.

Sella's diaries suggest that another reason for his not wanting to accompany the Duke on the Karakoram expedition may have been family responsibilities. An ancient family of the city of Biella, the Sellas had become prosperous as manufacturers of woolen garments. Sella's father, Guiseppe Venanzio wrote the first book on photography published in Italy, and his uncle Quintino had been minister of finance under the Duke's grandfather, King Vittorio Emanuele II. The family was proud of its achievements and its close association to members of the royal family. (The Sellas had once built an entire guest house and stable on the occasion of a three-day visit by King Umberto I to their estate.) At this time in his life Sella was much occupied in running, with his brother-in-law, the family's large estate in Sardinia and perhaps he felt it would not be appropriate for him to be absent from his duties for so long.

Sella was always deferential toward the Duke; Luigi di Savoia was after all his monarch, but the two men had become good friends. In his letters, Sella would address the Duke as "Altezza Reale" ("Royal Highness") and sign himself "col più affettuoso ossequio mi ripeto devotissimo, V.S." ("with most affectionate regards, I remain most devoted, V.S."). In turn, the Duke would address the photographer in his letters as "Caro Sella" ("Dear Sella") and sign them "Luigi di Savoia," or in later years, simply "Luigi."

Unfortunately, the Duke and Sella did not share an interest in art. Too polite to complain openly, Sella wrote about his frustrations in his diaries. In his notes on the Mount Saint Elias expedition, for example, Sella complained that the Duke "does not have an artistic temperament at all and the beauty of a view does not interest him." To Sella, his photography was far more than just scientific documentation—it was art.

Sella's artistic temperament often made him the odd man out. On the return journey from the Ruwenzori, Sella had been unhappy about stopping to hunt elephants with the Duke near Entebbe. Although Sella was a skilled hunter, he was weary of his companions' lack of appreciation for the scenery: "In spite of the alpinistic, geographic, and photographic success, it does not give me any satisfaction because of the daily disappointment about the sentiments and the moral quality of almost all of my companions, in whom you would not find a speck of poetry or of interest for the really beautiful things, should you look for it with a microscope."

We do not know from Sella's diaries and letters what finally led him to join the K2 expedition, but generations of climbers have been grateful for his decision. His photographs of the Karakoram range constitute not only a precious document for succeeding explorers and climbers, they are also among the most beautiful and thrilling images ever taken of the highest mountains on earth.

The Duke had little more than two months to gather the equipment for the expedition. Traveling incognito to London for expedition supplies under the name of Federico Negrotto, his aide-de-camp, he also spent hours poring over maps at the Royal Geographical Society and the Alpine Club. After acquiring more equipment as well as medical supplies in France, he returned to Italy just ahead of the newspaper reporters, who were still hunting for him in an attempt to find out who was responsible for the breakup of his romance with Katherine Elkins.

On March 26, without announcement or fanfare, the Duke and his companions sailed quietly from the port of Marseilles on the passenger ship *Oceana*, bound for Bombay.

The Karakoram, their ultimate destination, is a mountain range in the Kashmir region (now divided between India and Pakistan), which forms a natural barrier between India and China. It runs parallel to and north of the more familiar Himalayan ranges in Nepal and Tibet, which in 1909 were closed to foreigners. Only K2, the tallest peak in the range, and its satellite peaks remained available for climbing expeditions.

The Karakoram comprises the world's largest concentration of mountains and passes, including four 8,000-meter (26,247-foot) peaks within 15 miles (24 kilometers) of each other at the head of the Baltoro Glacier. Two more peaks are less than 100 meters (328 feet) short of 8,000 meters. Another nineteen peaks in this region rise to more than 7,600 meters (25,000 feet).

William Moorcraft, the first European explorer to visit the region in 1820, gave the mountain range the name of Karakoram, which means "Black Gravel" in Turkish. Between 1835 and 1861, a succession of European geographers and military expeditions explored the area. In 1887 Sir Francis Younghusband, a twenty-four-year-old British colonel in the 1st King's Dragoon Guards, arrived at the foot of the Karakoram chain. Younghusband had already made a thousand-mile traverse of Central Asia, traveling from Manchuria across the Gobi Desert as part of a military reconnaissance mission.

Despite having no guides and little climbing experience, Younghusband and his native bearers traversed the 18,000-foot (5,486-meter) Mustagh Pass, climbing without ice axes and wearing only native footgear. Younghusband used an ordinary pickax and feared they would all fall to their deaths at any moment. Incredibly, he led his party through a dangerous icefall to the safety of the Baltoro Glacier. Two years later, better equipped, Younghusband returned and explored the approaches to K2 from the northeast.

Younghusband's explorations had neither scientific nor mountaineering goals but were rather for the sake of political penetration. The first expedition with the express purpose of climbing was that of the British writer and art critic Martin Conway, who was backed by the Royal Geographical Society. In 1892, Conway explored and mapped three glaciers surrounding K2 and succeeded in climbing two peaks, 19,400-foot (5,913-meter) Crystal Peak and 22,867-foot (6,970-meter) Pioneer Peak. He also made an unsuccessful attempt at climbing 25,112-foot (7,654-meter) Bride Peak (Chogolisa). Conway's maps of the glaciers and Chogolisa were later used by the Duke in planning his expedition.

Perhaps the most prolific climbers of the Karakoram were the American physician and explorer William Hunter Workman and his wife, Fannie Bullock Workman.[14] During four expeditions in 1899, 1902, 1903, and 1908, they surveyed Karakoram glaciers and made many first ascents on several Karakoram peaks.

The information the Duke accumulated from the experiences of Conway and the Workmans led him to choose K2 as his destination. K2 (or Karakoram 2), as it was called by Captain T. G. Montgomerie of the Trigonometric Survey of India in 1856, was known to the local people as Chogori, meaning "great mountain." Given the best information of the day, Montgomerie concluded that Chogori was the second highest mountain in the world and logged it at 28,278 feet (8,619 meters) from a survey point 137 miles (221 kilometers) away. Its actual height is 28,250 feet (8,611 meters), a difference of only about 28 feet (7 meters) from Montgomerie's original observations.

Despite the explorations to the region, the Karakoram remained one of the least-known areas on earth, offering the Duke the opportunity to be the first to map much of the range. He had briefly considered the Sikkim Himalaya further to the east, but Douglas W. Freshfield had already mapped and studied this range in his circumnavigation of Kangchenjunga in 1899–1902. Vittorio Sella had accompanied Freshfield and had taken a wealth of photographs, later published in Freshfield's *Round Kangchenjunga: A Narrative of Mountain Travel and Exploration.*

The Duke had also considered launching an expedition to 26,660-foot (8,125-meter) Nanga Parbat, 125 miles (201 kilometers) to the west of K2, the largest and grandest of the 8,000-meter peaks in the western Punjab. By climbing Nanga Parbat, he could avenge his friend Mummery, who had died on the mountain. However, the Duke decided against the ascent, reasoning that there were no other peaks in the region to climb in case of failure on Nanga Parbat. More importantly, the Nanga Parbat region had been well mapped by previous parties, which meant that the Duke could make little in the way of new scientific contributions, always a primary consideration on his expeditions.

The Duke's principal reason for choosing K2 was his ambition of coming back to Italy with a first ascent and an altitude record. Announcing he would explore the "Third Pole" of altitude in the name of science, he was also keen to provide new medical information about what happens to the human body at high altitude.

In the Karakoram he could choose from an array of 25,000-foot (7,620-meter) peaks where he could both make a first ascent and surpass the altitude record set in October 1907 by the Norwegians Carl W. Rubenson and Monrad Aas, who had climbed the Kabru, near Jongri in the Sikkim Himalaya, reaching nearly 24,076 feet (7,338 meters). This mark exceeded Dr. Thomas G. Longstaff's altitude record of 23,360 feet (7,120 meters) on the summit of Trisul in the Garwhal Himalaya.

For the Duke of the Abruzzi, this expedition would be the greatest logistical challenge he had ever faced. Furthermore, the approach along the basin of the Baltoro Glacier would be more arduous than any he had yet attempted, with its snowy passes to surmount, turbulent rivers to ford, and vast desert zones to cross.

The preparations for the expedition pressed the Duke to the utmost of his resources. Sella's experience on Freshfield's Kanchenjunga expedition was invaluable, and the Duke designed tents made to withstand extremes of heat and cold. The Duke also designed sleeping bags made of four layers—

one of camel's hair, one of eiderdown, one of sheepskin, and an outer layer of waterproof canvas. Not one detail was neglected that could add comfort or safety.

Such were the demands of the long journey into the Karakoram and the difficulty of living for months in a hostile climate that only one previous group of climbers had gotten close enough to K2 to make an attempt. The Chogori expedition of 1902 consisted of a small group of men led by Oscar Eckenstein, a British rock climber who is credited with inventing the modern crampon and the short ice ax. Eckenstein was an outspoken advocate of guideless climbing, and his differences of opinion with the conservative Conway had resulted in his being expelled from the latter's 1892 expedition.

When Eckenstein tried to join other expeditions to the Himalaya, he was snubbed by members of the Alpine Club and so had founded a secessionist group, the Climbers' Club, whose members shared his noncomformist views. One of the climbing companions he invited on the Chogori expedition was Aleister Crowley, a boastful exhibitionist who was as critical of establishment climbers as they were of him.[15]

Eckenstein's expedition began badly. He was jailed in India on dubious charges, which led him to believe that Conway had used his influence to prevent him from surpassing Conway's altitude record. Released after a few days, Eckenstein was eventually able to rejoin his companions, who had proceeded under Crowley's leadership, only to find themselves underequipped, undermanned, and split by constant bickering.

The men of the expedition were a strange assortment of free-spirited and quarrelsome individualists. Under Crowley's command, tensions had increased, especially during long periods of confinement together in poor weather. In addition, Crowley had attempted to instill respect in the porters by beating them, whereupon they had deserted, taking with them some of the supplies. However, in spite of the difficulties, the expedition reached the base of K2.

At this point, Crowley wanted to attempt the summit in one day by the southeast ridge. Another member of the party, Jules Jacot-Guillarmod, a Swiss doctor who also wrote the expedition account, maintained that the summit could best be approached by way of a northeast spur.

A vote was taken, and Jacot-Guillarmod won. Setting off with Dr. V.

Wesseley, an Austrian, along the northeast crest in the middle of a snowstorm, he succeeded in reaching a small peak at 21,500 feet (6,553 meters) before being forced back by the weather.

Like Mummery on Nanga Parbat, Eckenstein and his companions were deceived by the scale of the mountain and had difficulty judging distances. A landmark that seemed at first only a few thousand feet away ended up taking several days to reach. Added to this was the defection of the porters, the discomfort and illnesses that affected almost everyone, the lack of supplies, and the general in-fighting. Lastly, the weather was terrible—of sixty-eight days on the mountain, only four were clear. Spent and bitter, Eckenstein called off the expedition. There would not be another attempt on K2 until that of the Duke in 1909.

The Duke studied Jacot-Guillarmod's accounts thoroughly, and the difficulties encountered by the Eckenstein expedition convinced him to take along a large contingent of Val d'Aosta mountaineers as porters and guides. He selected a quartet of guides: the father-and-son team of Joseph and Laurent Petigax and brothers Alexis and Henri Brocherel. The elder Petigax had been with the Duke on all his major expeditions, and both Petigax had been in the Karakoram with the Workmans on their 1903 expedition. The Brocherels had also had Himalayan experience on two expeditions led by Thomas Longstaff, including his ascent of Trisul in 1907. Supporting the guides were three porters, again Val d'Aosta men: Emile Brocherel, Albert Savoie, and Ernest Bareux.

The rest of the party consisted of, in addition to the Duke, Federico Negrotto, a trained topographer, who replaced Cagni as the Duke's aide-de-camp; Filippo De Filippi, who had served as expedition doctor and chronicler of the Mount Saint Elias expedition; Vittorio Sella; and Sella's assistant, Erminio Botta. These twelve men made up a small, well-attuned group capable of scaling mountain peaks, carrying out scientific studies, and of living together over a long period of time under difficult conditions.

The Duke had had good weather on both the Mount Saint Elias and the Ruwenzori expeditions and had made the summits on rare clear days. The K2 expedition would need vastly better luck. Both Eckenstein's and Conway's expeditions had endured terrible weather. In their four expeditions to the Karakoram, only once had the Workmans experienced two months of clear weather. After careful study, the Duke decided that the best time to begin the expedition was early June.

On March 13, the expedition and its baggage—132 pieces totaling 10,454 pounds (4,752 kilograms)—arrived by train at Rawalpindi. For the next several days, the five tons of gear and provisions were transported by hand-drawn cart and horse-drawn tonga over the wide dirt roads from Rawalpindi to Srinagar in the district of Kashmir.

Many of the customary delays were waived as the Italians' equipment crossed into Kashmir territory unimpeded on orders from the local representatives of the British government, Sir Francis and Lady Younghusband, who also staged a welcome for the Duke that included all the royal pomp and flourish the Srinagar community could muster.

When the expedition was ready to leave Srinagar, the Younghusbands saw them off with a royal escort of brightly decorated shikaras (river skiffs), each rowed by fifteen uniformed oarsmen. Crowds of the curious followed along the shore playing instruments, cheering, and throwing garlands of flowers into the canal.

At Younghusband's suggestion, while in Srinagar the Duke had hired A. C. Baines, an expedition organizer, to supervise the day-to-day hiring of porters and to arrange food and lodging along the way. Baines did his job well. He traveled a day or two ahead of the expedition with the luggage carried in horse-drawn carts, and by the time the Duke arrived in camp, it would be already set up, with tea waiting for him. All along the journey Baines arranged for festive events in the Duke's honor, and dignitaries from each town often lined up both to offer and to receive gifts.

On May 8 the expedition reached Skardu, where the men first caught sight of the giant peaks toward which they had been traveling. Having covered more than 225 miles (362 kilometers) of the western Himalaya in eleven days, the Duke called a halt in this enchanting village, surrounded by trees and rushing streams.

From the moment of the expedition's arrival, the town transformed itself to entertain them. The village chiefs organized a polo game in the Duke's honor and offered a banquet, but the weary climbers preferred to rest in the shade of the trees and recover from the heat of their arid journey. Here they were treated to dried fruits, sweet almonds and raisins, cakes, and fresh vegetables and entertained with music and dancing in a day of celebration that lasted well into the night.

Back in America, on May 2 the *New York Times* carried the first of several newspaper accounts of the Duke's expedition. Sharing the feature section that day was a story about Russia's Czar Nicholas, who was vacationing with his family on the Reba; a story about the beginning of the new baseball season; and another about the beginning of construction on the world's first unsinkable ocean liner. The *Times*, scant on facts, attributed the Duke's K2 expedition to his failed romance with Katherine Elkins and said that he had gone on a royal tiger hunt in India.

Quite the contrary, the Duke was covered in trail dust as he continued to journey toward the base of K2 with his usual escort of village chiefs. Upon the expedition's arrival at Skardu, they were treated to yet another polo match and offerings of delicacies, but the most welcome treats were again the few shade trees that gave the party some relief from the tortuous heat.

From Skardu, the route had been steadily rising in elevation, and by the time the expedition reached the hot springs in Askole, the temperature had dropped to 35 degrees Fahrenheit (1.7 degrees Celsius). The men had covered 295 miles (475 kilometers) in twenty-two days. Not once had there been a single mishap, nor had a single object been lost, a fact the Duke attributed more to the honesty of the Balti porters than to the efficiency of his organization.

From Askole, the party crossed the face of the Biafo Glacier, arriving on May 18 at the rough ground of the lower Baltoro Glacier. Here the ascent became more exhausting, especially for the 260 porters.

Baines welcomed the expedition at Rdokass (Urdukas), where he had already set up a base camp. From here he would supply the men with fresh milk, meat, and poultry. Having a constant source of fresh food assured the Italians that they would have enough for themselves and the porters. On the Eckenstein expedition, the porters had consumed all the food they were carrying before they reached the base of K2.

At the base camp, the Duke chose the 10 strongest porters to accompany the expedition to the highest camps and another 25 to carry equipment to the intermediate camps, outfitting them all with heavy garments, socks, snow glasses, boots, mittens, and sleeping bags. He left another 115 porters with Baines and discharged the rest with pay and provisions for their return journey.

The Italians closely followed the route taken by the Eckenstein expedition along the glacial moraine of the Baltoro. The rain had stopped and the wind had died down, though the skies remained cloudy, and on May 24 they made Camp I on broken and coarse detritus from the northern wall of the glacier. On May 25, the sky cleared, revealing Gasherbrum IV at the eastern end of the glacier. Turning north, the Italians came to Camp II in the Concordia amphitheater—so named by Conway because this junction of the Baltoro and Godwin Austen Glaciers resembles the amphitheater of the same name at the Aletsch Glacier in the Oberland Alps. Slowly, the veil of mist lifted, and at the other end of the glacier appeared the giant pyramid of K2. While Sella loaded some of the delicate plates into the Ross camera, the rest of the party looked at the mountain through field glasses, examining routes, comparing notes, and wrestling with their private doubts. Just before K2 disappeared again into its shroud of mist, Sella took his photograph.

The Duke set up Camp III on May 27 at the base of a southeast spur of the mountain and split the men into teams to make a reconnaissance. The results brought back to camp the next day were not encouraging. From base to summit, K2 rose 12,000 feet (3,658 meters). The eastern slopes were far too difficult, and the northeastern spur was impossibly steep, icy, and swept by constant avalanches. The only remaining option was a rib of rock that rose directly above Camp III, leading from the glacier to the shoulder of the mountain. This was the route originally suggested by Crowley on the Eckenstein expedition. It had the advantage of receiving the most sun from morning to evening and was the spur least exposed to the avalanches that swept every other part of the mountain. The Duke decided to attempt this route first.

On May 29 the weather cleared, and the men set their sights on a prominent point on the shoulder of the ridge. The Duke immediately realized that because of the altitude and the steepness of the climb, the porters' loads would have to be reduced. Sella, however, could not cut down on the weight of his equipment and so was asked by the Duke to stay at Camp III, thus freeing his porters for the climbers.

As storms raged on the summit, Joseph and Laurent Petigax, the Duke,

the three Italian porters, and a contingent of Balti porters set off up the southeast spur. On June 1, they set up Camp IV at 18,242 feet (5,560 meters).

After seeing falling rock on the slopes ahead of them, the Balti porters
threw down their loads and refused to leave their tents. The Duke stayed behind with them, while Joseph and Laurent Petigax and the Italian porters
continued on, installing fixed ropes across a difficult section of verglas and
mixed rock and snow to facilitate the next day's climb. However, when
Petigax returned to camp, he confessed to the Duke that he had grave
doubts about the route and that the continually falling snow was disorient-
ing. The party had made little progress in fixing the ropes because they had
had difficulty in determining the distance they had already climbed or the
distance before them. They had also suffered from baffling optical illusions:
sometimes they had thought they were on easy slopes only to find themselves facing perpendicular rock above and exposure below.

However, the next day, despite worsening weather, the two guides decided to try again. Reaching a couloir where they had placed ropes the day
before, they noticed a reddish rock band on a shoulder leading in the direction of the summit. The wall was steep and exposed, and they could see that,
even with a fixed rope, this vertical route would be too difficult for the Balti
porters to climb. On the other hand, they were still too far from the summit to
think of doing without the tents, provisions, and other supplies the porters
carried. Petigax, never one to turn back if there was the slightest possibility of
success, decided to go no farther.

Returning to Camp IV, they reported their findings to the Duke, who
called off the attempt. They had reached an altitude of between 20,341 feet
(6,200 meters) and 21,981 feet (6,700 meters). From this time forward, the
southeast ridge of K2 would be known as the Abruzzi Spur. Greatly disappointed, the climbers returned to Camp III, where their spirits were revived
by Baines's latest supply of fresh meat, eggs, and milk.

The first attempt had failed, but the expedition was not over. As soon as
it stopped snowing, the Duke led a new attempt on a broad ice saddle on the
west side of K2, which he had noted on his initial reconnaissance, hoping
that from there it would be possible to reach the northwest spur of the
mountain.

Once again the party was misled by the easy appearance of the route.

The glacier was steep, full of crevasses, and coursed with avalanches. At this altitude, the sun was blinding, and the lack of oxygen made every step painful. The men's progress toward the top of the saddle was very slow.

The party continued the ascent, but at 21,870 feet (6,666 meters), they saw that they were cut off from the northern slopes of K2 by a corniced ridge. After the twelve hours of exhausting climbing they had already done that day attacking such a cornice would be difficult, if not impossible. Disappointed, they set up camp (Camp V) on the glacier which, along with the col, was given the name Savoia.

Up until this point the expedition had not experienced more than three consecutive days of fine weather. The nights were freezing; by day the wind blew snow and slivers of ice in their faces, making climbing impossible. They had made two attempts on the mountain and had been driven back each time. With no sign that the weather would improve, the Duke decided to give up on K2 and to explore instead the upper basin of the Godwin Austen Glacier.

On June 16, the Duke reached Camp VI, located at the foot of the northeast spur of K2. From here he would attempt 24,752-foot (7,544-meter) Skyang Kangri, or Staircase Peak.

In the meantime, Sella had already started in this direction, intending to climb a pass east of K2 from which he counted on seeing—and photographing—the mountains of China. With the help of Botta and Negrotto, Sella succeeded in transporting his large tent-laboratory and all his photographic equipment, including glass plates and chemical emulsions, to the top of the pass (which the Duke would later name Sella Pass in his honor). The sky was cloudless, and Sella was able to take panoramic photographs of the eastern walls of the giant Gasherbrum group and Broad Peak. The good weather also permitted him to take a shot of China's Teram Kangri, which Longstaff was then exploring.

These extraordinary photographs cost Sella, Botta, and Negrotto much in labor and fatigue. Again and again they had to set up and take down the tents and prepare the photographic equipment for use—sheltering it from the wind and protecting it from the reflection of the sun. Finally, the three men made camp (Camp VII) at the far end of the Godwin Austen Glacier, which Eckenstein had named Windy Gap.[16]

The next day, Sella succeeded in photographing K2 from the east. From his viewpoint, the southeast ridge, which the Duke and his guides had at-tempted, appeared as a sheer wall of ice, crowned by seracs. The awesome sight led Sella to believe the mountain would never be climbed.

On June 17, the Duke, climbing with both Petigax, Alexis and Emile Brocherel, and Albert Savoie, began the relatively easy ascent up the gentle slopes of an ice rib leading to Staircase Peak. Soon, however, Alexis Brocherel, who had earlier fallen into a crevasse and injured his ribs, had to retreat down the glacier, accompanied by Emile Brocherel and Savoie. The rest of the party continued to climb rapidly but it began to snow so heavily that they could see nothing and also had to retreat to Camp VII.

A few days later, when the sky had cleared, the Duke and the two Petigax set out again. They were making rapid progress toward the second step of the plateau when their way was blocked by an ice wall on the right and large crevasses on the left. At this point, they were all fatigued and be-ginning to suffer the effects of altitude, and the Duke was falling behind. For the third time on the expedition, he declared himself defeated and made Camp VIII at 21,657 feet (6,601 meters).

It was a poor consolation for the Duke that he was able to take advan-tage of a momentary clearing in the weather to take a stunning photograph of K2 from the southern ridge of Staircase Peak. The Duke's photograph—in Sella's words, as good as any he himself had taken on the journey—was later published as the frontispiece of the expedition book, where it was erro-neously attributed to Sella.

At Mount Saint Elias and in the Ruwenzori, the weather had been kind to the Duke, but at K2 it had been no better for him than it had been for Eckenstein. Believing he had just a few days of fair weather still left on the expedition, the Duke felt it was not worthwhile staying any longer at K2 and decided to try his luck at the southern end of the Karakoram. The expe-dition had completed the mapping of the upper Baltoro Glacier, as well as numerous botanical and geologic observations, and Sella had taken a wealth of photographs. But the Duke would not be satisfied until the expedition had attained a record: if they could not conquer a peak, they would at least claim an altitude record.

As an objective, the Duke chose the as-yet unclimbed 25,112-foot

(7,654-meter) Bride Peak (Chogolisa), located in the middle of the Golden Throne group, which forms the far southern wall of the Baltoro Glacier and was named for its reflection of bright golden light at sunset. Unsuccessfully attempted by Conway in 1892, Bride Peak would offer the Duke both a first ascent and an altitude record.

On July 1, the Duke set up base camp (Camp XI) at 16,637 feet (5,071 meters), at a spot near Conway's camp. His experience on K2 had made him much more cautious about his plans, and he selected a route that would allow the inexperienced Balti porters to carry loads much of the way—over the glacier toward the east face of the peak and up to a saddle that followed the crest to the summit. He estimated that it would take two days to reach the saddle.

On July 4, the Duke attacked the route with Vittorio Sella and the four guides. Several times they had to cross difficult stretches strewn with seracs, yawning dark caverns, and great bottomless crevasses reminiscent of the Newton Glacier on Mount Saint Elias, which the Duke, Joseph Petigax, Sella, and Botta had traversed twelve years earlier, almost to the day.

They set up Camp XII at 17,959 feet (5,474 meters)—1,322 feet (402 meters) above base camp—on the only flat surface in the middle of the tortuous glacier.

The next day they encountered the same tough going as Conway had in 1892. The Duke returned to Camp XII exhausted while Sella, with four guides, and seven fully loaded Balti porters continued on, establishing Camp XIII at 19,098 feet (5,821 meters). Here they were forced to wait out a storm that lasted two days.

The Duke sent a porter up to Camp XIII with a note saying that the snow conditions were getting dangerous and the group should return to the camp below. Realizing his chances of taking any photographs or making any progress up the mountain would be difficult under the circumstances, Sella descended. He would not return. He spent the rest of the expedition in a solitary makeshift camp on the Baltoro Glacier; here he produced panoramic views that are now considered to be among his finest works.

When the weather finally improved, the Duke and four guides continued the ascent, climbing slowly in fresh snow up to their knees and finally up to their waists until they reached Camp XIII just 1,686 feet (514 meters) below the saddle.

On July 10, nine days after setting up base camp and the only clear day on the climb, the expedition reached the saddle at 20,784 feet (6,335 meters). Before setting up Camp XIV, the Duke sent the seven exhausted Balti porters and the four guides back to base camp, leaving himself, Joseph Petigax, and Henri and Emile Brocherel to witness a spectacular view of K2 at sunset, the only clear view of the massif and surrounding peaks they would see on the entire journey.

With the summit just over 4,326 feet (1,318 meters) away, the four men continued to climb in waist-deep snow and bivouacked at Camp XV at 21,673 feet (6,606 meters). On July 12, after climbing for several hours in dense fog, they had reached an altitude of 23,458 feet (7,150 meters) when a storm broke, and they decided to descend to Camp XIV because of the danger from the overhanging cornices and frequent avalanches. Here they were forced to remain in their two cramped Mummery tents for four days, walled in by a snowstorm. They emerged again on July 17 and succeeded in placing another camp (Camp XVbis) only 2,625 feet (800 meters) below the summit.

On July 18, in the worst snow yet, they set off again at 5:30 A.M. and easily reached the top of the shoulder at 23,000 feet (7,010 meters). Just as before, however, a dense mist closed in around them, obscuring the route entirely.

They continued to climb above the shoulder for another four and a half hours along a knife-edged crest with a series of cornices on one side and open crevasses on the other. To avoid the crevasses they had to walk dangerously near to the cornices, which threatened to collapse under their feet from one moment to the next. Measuring the altitude, they found they were at 24,275 feet (7,399 meters), a new altitude record.

Before them were insidious rocks covered with verglas. The Duke naturally wanted the summit, and by luck, once they were over the rocks, they were able to ascend a snowy slope without difficulty. They continued to climb in the ever-thickening fog until at last they were forced to stop. They waited for two and a half hours, and still the fog gave no sign of thinning. A new reading with their Fortrin barometer showed that they were at 24,600 feet (7,498 meters), surpassing the altitude record of Rubenson and Aas by 524 feet (160 meters).

The Duke would have liked to continue on to the summit, but it was impossible to see the route in front of them, and since it was getting late, he decided to descend. He was disappointed in not making the summit, but it was a less painful defeat than the previous ones on K2. He would be taking home an altitude record, which would remain unbeaten until the British attempt on Everest from Tibet thirteen years later in 1922.

Several more expeditions would come to conquer K2, including one led by Luigi de Savoia's nephew, the Duke of Spoleto, twenty years later in 1929. Fittingly, the first to stand on the summit of K2 would be the Italians Achille Compagnoni and Lino Lacedelli, who reached the summit on July 31, 1954, by way of the Abruzzi Spur—forty-five years after the Duke's attempt.

Chogolisa's corniced ridge, which had caused the Duke's expedition so much anxiety, claimed the life of the legendary Hermann Buhl in 1957. Buhl had climbed with Kurt Diemberger to 23,950 feet (7,300 meters), and they were descending unroped during a sudden snowstorm when Buhl disappeared over the jagged edge of the ridge. Chogolisa would finally be conquered in 1958 by a Japanese expedition, which took a route along the crest of the northeast summit. The southwest summit was claimed by an Austrian team in 1975.

Scientifically, the expedition was a success. Among other things, the Duke had disproved William Workman's assertion that man was not able to spend the night at altitudes more than 20,000 feet (6,096 meters). The Duke, his guides, and the Balti porters had all lived for thirty-seven days above 16,000 feet (4,877 meters), nine of those days having been spent above 21,000 feet (6,401 meters). And although the Duke did not make any specific studies on altitude sickness, he observed that, apart from minor maladies, only one man had shown signs of real illness during the expedition's long periods at these high altitudes.

At the end of July, the Duke's expedition was finished. Waiting for the men at Rdokass was mail from home, including several newspaper articles. Of particular interest to the Duke was the news that over the summer, both Frederick Cook and Peary claimed to have reached the North Pole. The Duke announced that they must leave for Italy immediately so that he could report their successes to the king without delay.

When the ship carrying the expedition home from India stopped in Port Said on the way back into the Mediterranean, reporters clambered aboard to interview the Duke. More than details of the expedition, they were eager to know if it was true that he was going to proceed from Marseilles to Paris for a meeting with Katherine Elkins. That summer, several newspaper articles had appeared in which Miss Elkins had been shown vacationing in Paris in the company of the American Billy Hitt.

After giving the reporters a brief account of the highlights of the expedition, the Duke excused himself brusquely. For the rest of the voyage he passed the greater part of the time alone, seated in the music room, closed in an impenetrable silence. No doubt he found it galling to once again be in the newspapers as the subject of gossip rather than as a hero of exploration. In contrast to his exuberance on his return from previous expeditions, this time he made no pretense at celebration.

Chapter Eight

❦

The War Years

THE DUKE RETURNED TO AN ITALY IN THE THROES OF CHANGE. A NEW movement known as Futurism was all the rage among the intelligentsia. The Futurists' inflammatory manifesto, authored by Filippo Tommaso Marinetti and published in 1910, gave voice to their aspirations for an ideal world in which all that represented the past would be destroyed.

We wish to sing the love of danger, the habit of energy and temerity. Courage, boldness, rebellion shall be the essential elements of our poetry. Heretofore literature has exalted pensive stillness, rapture, and sleep. We wish to glorify aggressive movement, feverish restlessness, the running pace, the death-defying leap, the slap, the punch. We assert that the magnificence of the world has enriched itself with a new beauty: the beauty of speed. A racing car adorned with great pipes like serpents with explosive breath, a roaring automobile that seems to run over grapeshot, is more beautiful than the Victory of Samothrace. . . . There is no beauty except in combat. No work without aggressive character can be a masterpiece. . . . We want to glorify war—sole hygiene in the world—militarism, patriotism, the destructive zest of libertarians, the beautiful ideals for which it is worth dying, and the scorn of women.

However, behind this high-sounding rhetoric, an obscure and disquieting theme insinuated itself into the new ideology: a true disavowal of the principles of social justice that had characterized previous intellectual movements in Italy as well as in the rest of Europe. Suddenly swept away were all the humanitarian doctrines that had contributed to the social progress of the nineteenth century.

This new wave of warlike sentiment played into the hands of nationalists whose sole aim was to put Italy among the dominant nations conquering colonial territories in Africa. Caught up in Marinetti's bold rhetoric, intellectuals and politicians conveniently forgot the disasters suffered in Africa only a few decades earlier.

After Italy's ignominious defeat at Adwa in 1896, her colonial ambitions came to an abrupt halt. All that remained of her territories were two meager possessions on the harsh, rocky soil of the Horn of Africa: a small settlement in the isolated desert coastal region of Eritrea and a protectorate in Somaliland, where fewer than twenty Italians had lived since the region first came under Italy's jurisdiction in 1905.

There was not much of Africa left to choose from, however, because England, France, Germany, and Belgium had taken the lion's share of the continent. In 1881 France had taken over Tunisia, and Germany was looking for another country to add to its sizable possessions across Africa. Only a few desert areas remained available for occupation, and these would be lost if Italy did not act quickly.

In this atmosphere of renewed colonial fever the Duke returned to active naval duty, receiving his long-awaited promotion to rear admiral and command of the Royal Arsenal at Venice on November 19, 1909. His official duties became more and more oppressive, and it was not easy to find the time to prepare the Karakoram expedition account. The compilation of the material was entrusted to De Filippi, but as with the preceding expedition books, all the phases of drafting and production were done by the Duke with the collaboration of Vittorio Sella. It was two years before the massive two-volume edition containing the narrative account, as well as reports on all the scientific observations and surveys, was published.

The Duke's military obligations also prevented him from accepting numerous requests to lecture on the expedition. He presented his only official report before the Italian Alpine Club in Turin on February 16, 1910, and later published an article on the expedition in the newsletter of the Italian Geographic Society.

That winter, the newspapers were still busy with the story of Katherine Elkins, reporting that she had remained in contact with the Duke and had even met him in Paris after his return from the Karakoram. The *New York Times* continued to speak of the engagement as if there had been no official denial. By this time, however, the Duke was resigned to the excesses of the press and made sure he was seen in public as little as possible. Gradually, even the most tenacious journalists let the subject drop, and the Duke's romance was at least temporarily forgotten.

Senator Elkins had also disappeared from public view that year. In spite of reports that he was being considered as the Republican nominee for president, he was spending most of his time at Halliehurst, where it was said he was recuperating from a stomach ailment. On December 5, 1910, he appeared before reporters at Halliehurst to say that he was well on the road to recovery, but one month later, at midnight on January 4, 1911, he was dead. His friends blamed the senator's death on his distress over newspaper speculations about the scandals in which he had supposedly been involved, and on the hostility of public opinion, which held him responsible for the failure of his daughter's engagement.

The colonial ambitions of the government of Prime Minister Giovanni Giolitti—supported by the right-wing nationalists, the Church, the Bank of Rome, and numerous industrialists—were focused on a Turkish possession in north Africa: Cyrenaica, which Italy rebaptized Libya, its name under the Roman Empire.

Italy did not want to inherit this desert colony as a museum piece of its ancient past but rather to build there, along Italy's "fourth shore," a modern empire that would rival the Libya of the Romans. Italian businessmen were already trading with the territory, importing ivory, ostrich feathers, and mineral ores. It seemed that all that was needed to take possession of Libya was a brief war with Turkey, whose Ottoman Empire was already greatly weakened.

In the meantime, Italian diplomats hurried to make secret treaties with France and England to ensure that they would not intervene in the case of war with Turkey. This was not a simple matter, for Italy was still considered by its neighbors to be an immature and overly ambitious nation "with a very large appetite and very poor teeth," as Germany's chancellor Otto von Bismarck had scornfully remarked in reference to Italy's limited military force.

In 1911, the Italian navy was still in a position of inferiority in respect to the fleets of other European powers, chiefly because of its constrained finances, which forced it to skimp on maintenance so that only a small number of ships were operational at any time. Low pay, lack of pensions, and slow advancement in rank hindered recruitment, and the navy suffered from a lack of experienced officers just when it was most in need of them. At international conferences, Italian naval officers were humiliated to be relegated to the lowest order of protocol. Often they were not even consulted on important matters by their own allies, Germany and Austria.[17]

As the time for renewal of its treaty with Germany and Austria approached, Italy hoped to improve its position in the Triple Alliance by proving its worth as a major European power. A victorious war against Turkey for the possession of Libya would serve the purpose, but the Italians also needed to strengthen their fleet if their navy was to command respect in the court of European opinion.

At thirty-six, the Duke appeared much younger, and without his chevrons and medals, no one would have taken him for a rear admiral. Despite a carefully cultivated mustache and his naturally serious demeanor, he seemed out of place among his gray-bearded foreign colleagues. His reputation, however, was another matter. He was accustomed to command in the most difficult situations, and the success of his expeditions had given him a cachet that few officers in the world could boast. His promotion to rear admiral was a winning card in Italy's play for international respect.

In the course of thirty years in the service of the navy, the Duke had witnessed the decline of his country as a naval power. Between 1870 and 1880, Italy had ranked with the other Great Powers—at a certain point, in third place behind the navies of Great Britain and France—but it had now fallen to seventh place. While Germany and Austria were rapidly arming themselves with new warships, and the developing industrial powers of Japan and the United States were building large, modern navies almost overnight, Italy was struggling with political and economic chaos and desperately imposing taxes and appropriations to build new vessels and maintain its aging fleet.

In June 1909, while the Duke was climbing in the Karakoram, Italy had finally launched the first of four dreadnoughts that would make up the strength of its renovated fleet: the 19,500-ton *Dante Alighieri*.[18] It was a year ahead of Austria in this respect, but because of slow delivery of materials, incomplete weapons fittings, and engineering mistakes, the *Dante Alighieri* would have to wait another two years before being ready for combat.

With nearly every nation in Europe locked in an arms race, each navy became so caught up in an engineering frenzy that their commanding officers had no time to consider how the existence of heavily armored, high-speed battleships had altered the fundamental strategies of naval warfare.

In 1911, Turkey had nothing in the way of powerful dreadnoughts operating in the Adriatic or anywhere else. Its naval force consisted mostly of small, fast torpedo boats designed for surprise attacks from the shelter of the Adriatic islands and inlets along the Dalmatian coast.

The Duke was assigned to patrol a 217-mile (350-kilometer) strip of Albanian coastline to prevent Turkish attacks on Italian transports headed for Libya via the Straits of Otranto at the heel of Italy's boot. He was also to secure the lines of communication and to protect the lengthy Italian coastline.

Meanwhile, European diplomats urged Italy to pull away from the brink of war with Turkey, warning that a further weakening of the Ottoman Empire might allow the continuing conflict between Muslims and Serbs in the Balkans to get out of hand, and that this could lead to a full-scale war if the European allies of the various factions got involved. Aware of the consequences of just such an action, the moderate Giolitti presented the issue to the Italian parliament: Were they certain that a war against Turkey would not set off an uncontrollable chain of conflicts? Were they really ready to put a match to powder?

The Parliament was still debating these questions when it recessed at the end of August. With the government on holiday, the king and his advisors demanded that Turkey relinquish Libya. No answer was immediately forthcoming, and finally Italy issued an ultimatum, set to expire at 2:00 P.M. on September 29, 1911, that Turkey should withdraw from the African colony or face war.

The morning of September 29 found the Duke and the fleet under his command (two squadrons of destroyers) positioned off the coast of Epirus (now part of Greece) near the port of Préveza at the mouth of the Gulf of

Arta. His orders were rather confusing: in the case of attack, he was to make a threat of force without actually firing on enemy vessels.

War had not yet been declared when the Italian commanders learned that Turkish patrol craft were gathering at the entrance to the Gulf of Arta and were evidently preparing for an attack on the Italian ships.

Waiting on board his flagship, the *Vettor Pisani*, an old cruiser, the Duke became increasingly concerned over the vague and contradictory reports he was receiving from the Ministry of the Navy. He felt that war was imminent and inevitable and that he must prepare for battle. He sent Captain Guido Biscaretti on the *Artigliere* and Captain Italo Ricci on the *Alpino* to lie in wait outside the port. If the Turkish ships ventured out toward the open sea to confront the Italian forces, it would be considered an act of hostility, but if the Turkish vessels withdrew, there would be no battle.

The first shots were fired at 2:45 P.M. on September 29. The sky was clear and the sea was calm as two Turkish torpedo craft cleared the harbor of Préveza, heading for the Italian destroyers. When they failed to turn back, Ricci ordered the firing of the *Alpino's* guns, and Biscaretti on the *Artigliere* followed suit.

One of the Turkish boats, the *Tokat*, was hit. It made an about-face and tried to reach the safety of the port but caught fire, whereupon its crew threw themselves overboard and sought to escape by swimming to shore. Many of them reached land, but others were picked up by the Italian ships. The second Turkish torpedo craft, the *Eliagot*, succeeded in making it safely back into the harbor.

Several of the Turkish officers taken on board as prisoners inadvertently said too much in arrogance, and Biscaretti learned of additional Turkish ships at the port of Hegoumenitsa north of Préveza, including a destroyer and another vessel masquerading as a tourist ship that was, in fact, armed. Both were flying the Ottoman flag.

Worried, the Duke sent Biscaretti to check out the accuracy of this information, and the *Artigliere* was fired upon while still standing off Hegoumenitsa. Undamaged by the attack, the *Artigliere* replied by launching a torpedo, disabling the Turkish destroyer. The tourist ship surrendered quickly at the first shot from the *Artigliere*. It was indeed armed.

Seeing an opportunity to capture the rest of the Turkish fleet in port, the Duke commanded Biscaretti to proceed south through the Straits of Corfu.

However, with total victory within his grasp, the Duke received orders from the minister of the navy, Admiral Leonardi Cattolica, to pull back his ships.

The Duke wired Cattolica back, arguing that the offensive should be continued while the Turkish vessels were still in port and vulnerable to attack; otherwise, his own ships would be put in jeopardy. When Cattolica did not answer, the Duke ordered his flagship back to the naval base at Taranto to plead his case with the admiral directly. Their meeting was a failure: Cattolica ordered the Duke to patrol the area but not to engage the enemy before receiving precise orders to do so.

In the Duke's absence, Biscaretti continued his circuit along the Albanian coast past Valona (Vlorë), Durazzo (Durrës), and San Giovanni di Medua. At Medua he sighted numerous Turkish ships in harbor, including a steamer sailing under the Austrian flag. Hoisting a white flag on the *Artigliere*, he approached the Austrian steamer, asking permission to carry out an inspection to ascertain whether it was transporting Turkish arms. He had not yet reached the Austrian ship when suddenly heavy artillery fire rained upon the *Artigliere* from the shore, hitting the vessel broadside. The *Artigliere* returned fire and quickly withdrew.

Biscaretti was wounded in the foot by a shell burst and had to be evacuated to the port of Brindisi, where he reported to the Duke that in Medua he had detected a Turkish force of at least a thousand men, armed with six mortars and five or more machine-gun emplacements.

Biscaretti's report of Turkish troops at Medua was met with skepticism by the Italian government, provoking an angry response from the Duke, who defended Biscaretti and denounced the impracticality of the orders he had received from Rome. He also sent a sharply worded message to his superiors saying that Italy was finally in a position to assure its supremacy in the Adriatic and that it was time to act. His words, however, fell on deaf ears, and he received no reply. Rather than wait, he ordered his naval patrols to continue.

On October 4, the Duke's squadrons found several Turkish ships in harbor at Préveza, and the Duke requested permission to send an ultimatum to the Turkish commander to surrender or risk bombardment. He further suggested to his superiors that Italy should bombard all Adriatic ports with Turkish ships in harbor until they surrendered. For the next twenty-four hours, the Duke waited for a response from the ministry, his frustration building as he watched the opportunity for a decisive engagement slip away.

On the following day, the Duke received a cryptic message from Rome stating: "Since the Albanian coast has been completely explored, political considerations demand that surveillance be kept from outside the Adriatic." The Duke was ordered to abandon his position immediately and to patrol the area between Cape Matapan on the Greek Peloponnesus and Candia on Crete, as well as the Corinth Canal, to prevent Turkish torpedo boats from entering the Adriatic and attacking the convoys transporting Italian troops to Tripoli.

To the Duke it appeared that the Italian government had suddenly reversed its course. It was loath to win the battle for which it had campaigned so long.

Unbeknownst to the Duke, his actions at Hegoumenitsa and Préveza had caused an international controversy over who had fired the first shots of the war and whether the battle had come before or after the declaration of war. The Turkish government maintained that Italy was in breach of international treaties.

From Ricci's reports it appears that he opened fire at 2:45 P.M., and since Italy's ultimatum to Turkey expired at 2:00 P.M., the action of the Italian fleet was lawful. Nevertheless, it was still interpreted as an act of aggression by most European nations. In addition, Austria, worried that a decisive Italian victory in the Adriatic would instigate a war of liberation against the Turks in Dalmatia, called upon Italy to cease all hostilities.

Commander Biscaretti was accused of having disobeyed orders by opening fire too soon and seizing ships. The Duke defended him, charging that the ministry's orders were never explicit and often contradictory. He further maintained that he had preferred to be reprimanded than to wait lamely for orders while putting ships and men in danger. Despite the Duke's intervention, Biscaretti was discharged and the Duke himself received a reprimand. However, the Duke continued to insist that the military command should not be subordinated to political orders, and his relations with the government remained strained.

The torpedo boats under the Duke's command were subsequently assigned to escort Italian convoys to Libya and to intercept the transport of military supplies to the Turkish troops in Cyrenaica. During a respite in the fighting, the navy was planning a demonstrative action in the Dardanelles and an attack on the Turkish-held Dodecanese islands, which began in the first days of May. The Duke participated actively in this operation, visiting numerous anchorages on board the *Pisani* and assisting General Amelio, commander in chief of the occcupation of Rodi, in the choice of points of embarkation for the Italian troops.

On May 23, the Duke was promoted to vice admiral, and on June 26 he was assigned to the highest position of command at La Spezia, appointments that helped mend the relations between the Italian government and the joint naval forces. The next year, he received from the king the decoration of the Military Order of Savoy.

Major glory came to the Duke's friend Captain Umberto Cagni in another theater of the war. On October 5 Cagni disembarked at Tripoli with 1,732 marines. Occupying strategic points, Cagni and his men held their positions for six days against the Turkish forces before the arrival of reinforcements. The Italian press celebrated Cagni as a hero, calling him "the Garibaldi of the sea," and Vittorio Emanuele III conferred on him the title of Count of Bumeliana.

Despite all the optimistic predictions, the war in Libya was not brief. Notwithstanding ninety thousand troops, superiority at sea, and the ability to bomb from the air in a new weapon called the airplane, the Italian army could not win a decisive victory over the Turks. More Italians were dying of cholera than battle wounds, and Italy found itself mired in a war it would never win.

Above all, Italy never obtained the respect it desired among the Great Powers. On the contrary, Italy's notorious colonial incompetence and the certainty with which it had claimed it would be able to conquer Libya in three weeks were an ironic joke in the capitals of Europe. Rumors of atrocities committed by Italian soldiers against Libyan civilians circulated in the foreign press, and instead of adding to Italy's glory, the war ended up tarnishing its reputation even further.

The Libyan War finally ended seven months later on November 11, 1912, with the Treaty of Ouchy, which officially annexed Libya to Italy. The next twenty years, however, were filled with revolts and guerrilla warfare on the part of the Libyan populations of Senussians and Bedouins, who had fought for independence against the Turks and continued to fight against the Italians. The long series of rebellions, attacks, and skirmishes ended only with the invasion of Mussolini's troops in 1931.

If Italy's reputation suffered from the Libyan War, the Duke's fame continued to soar. As the European naval commander most experienced in modern naval warfare, he was a sought-after speaker at international delegations, diplomatic cruises, and naval staff conferences across Europe. His decisive action in the Adriatic had also gained him the further respect of Kaiser Wihelm II, who invited him, along with King Vittorio Emanuele III, to Kielerwoche, an annual week-long regatta at Kiel instituted by the Kaiser as the German equivalent of his uncle King Edward VII's annual regatta at Cowes, England.

The Austrians had not forgiven Italy for its "disobedience" in the Adriatic, but that did not prevent them from personally admiring the Duke for the very actions that had cost him his assignment. In fact, when Italy, Germany, and Austria finally met to renew their Triple Alliance naval treaty in 1913, it was Austria who proposed the Duke as the supreme commander of the Allied naval forces. His praises were even sung by Emperor Franz Joseph, who remarked: "There is a capable leader."

For reasons historians have still not been able to fathom, the Duke's candidacy was acceptable to everyone but the Italian delegation, and the position was eventually given to an Austrian. Upon learning of this outcome, the Duke once again felt betrayed by his superiors.

In the aftermath of the Libyan war, the Duke set about reviving his personal life. He continued to keep in contact with Vittorio Sella, who was a prolific letter writer. Over time Sella's letters had become more informal and friendly. He often expressed his joy when the Duke was given a new command, and he showed his displeasure when his friend was forced to leave the Adriatic assignment. The two men would not meet again to climb in the Alps, however. Sella's health had declined, and in one letter he wrote: "The season for alpine ascents has been bad and continues to be grim, but I am not unhappy because I consider myself dead to mountaineering anyway."

After a long absence from high society, the Duke reentered a life of intense social activity in the fall of 1913. He was spotted giving directions to American tourists on the streets of Rome; he served as an interpreter for a visiting American diplomatic mission; he won a tango contest in Venice (and was later reproved by the clerical press for having introduced that sinful dance into Italy). In October he took part in the centennial celebrations of the birth of composer Guiseppe Verdi, and when he arrived to take his seat at a performance of La Traviata, the entire audience rose to applaud him.

Once again the newspapers began to speak of Katherine and the Duke, taking up the lingering rumor that he could marry anyone he chose if he were to become king of Albania. When it was later learned that King Vittorio Emanuele III had made a secret deal with Austria to crown the Prince of Wied, an Austrian, as king of Albania, the Italian papers condemned the decision as yet another rebuke of the Duke that was based on jealousy. The Duke would not speak about Katherine with the press except to say that he had written "to release her from her engagement," and that there was now no possibility of marriage.

Meanwhile, perhaps feeling uneasy about the Duke's career misfortunes, or perhaps pushed by his mother, Vittorio Emanuele III entrusted to the Duke the command of the navy's First Squadron. On October 21, 1913, Vice Admiral Luigi di Savoia raised anchor and left the port of Genoa aboard the Regina Elena for a cruise in the eastern Mediterranean.

On October 31, the press reported the marriage of Katherine Elkins to Billy Hitt, which had taken place three days earlier. According to the news stories, Katherine, after receiving a cable from the Duke, called her family together at Halliehurst, where she and Billy Hitt were married in the drawing room by a local town minister, who conducted a brief ceremony.

As predicted by Austria, the decline of the Ottoman Empire had the effect of destablizing the rebellious Balkans. Bosnia and Herzegovina were in tumult, and on June 28, 1914, the Archduke Ferdinand, heir to the Austrian throne, was shot and killed by a nineteen-year-old Bosnian while visiting Sarajevo on a goodwill mission with his wife. The assassin, Gavrilo Princip, was affiliated with the Black Hand, a militant group of Serbian nationalists dedicated to the separation of Serbia and the other Slav provinces from the Austro-Hungarian Empire and to the creation of the kingdom of Greater Serbia.

The assassination of Archduke Ferdinand was the match that lit the great conflagration of World War I. Backed by Germany, Austria moved against the Serbians. Russia took sides with Serbia, and France with Russia. Great Britain entered the conflict on the side of France when Germany invaded Belgium. Italy, however, did not immediately join the fray. The Triple Alliance treaty, renegotiated in 1913, allowed Italy to remain neutral if its allies began a war against Serbia or Great Britain. Furthermore, Italy had also signed an agreement with France acknowledging Italy's right to non-belligerence in case of war.

Prime Minister Giolitti had been forced to resign at the beginning of 1914, and the new prime minister, Antonio Salandra, found the Italian government woefully unprepared to finance a war.[19] The Libyan War had dried up the country's finances, and its troops were still fighting rebellions in Libya. Not surprisingly, the vast majority of war-weary Italians supported neutrality.

Only a small minority were in favor of entering the war on the side of Austria. The new, industrial Italy depended on Great Britain for coal and raw material, while between Italy and France there existed an ancient bond of cultural affinity apart from any economic concerns. Everything indicated that if Italy were to enter the war, it would be allied with France and Great Britain against Austria and Germany.

However, despite the popular sentiment against a European war, an aggressive nationalist and interventionist movement had the upper hand. On April 26, 1915, Italy repudiated the Triple Alliance treaty and on May 10 signed the Treaty of London, thereby officially joining the Triple Entente of England, France, and Russia.

Upon Italy's entry into the war, Luigi di Savoia was named commander in chief of the joint naval forces in the Adriatic, and the entire Aosta family took its place at the front. Emanuele Filiberto, the Duke's eldest brother, commanded the Third Army. Vittorio Emanuele, the Duke's second eldest brother, became the general inspector of the cavalry. His youngest brother, Umberto Maria, was a captain in the infantry, and his nephews, the two young sons of Emanuele Filiberto, also enlisted in the infantry. The royal family's devotion to duty, in this, perhaps the least desired, but most horrendous war in all of Italy's history, was above reproach. Even the king, despite his repugnance for military life, spent long periods in the trenches, dressed in the gray-green uniform of a soldier and sleeping in a tent—winning, if not the affection, at least the respect of the troops.

The Duke's first task was to modify the naval strategies prepared by his predecessors for a war that they had expected to be against France and Great Britain. Now Italy's former enemies were its allies, but both France and Great Britain mistrusted Italy, which, for reasons that are still unclear, had not yet declared war on Germany.

At age forty-two, the Duke was faced with the most difficult task of his life, that of creating a unified battle strategy for three fleets that spoke different languages, maintained separate operational structures, and held fast to different strategies for winning the war. The French, under Vice Admiral Augustin Boué de Lapeyrère, wanted to pursue a large-ship strategy and bombard the Austrian positions to force Austria into a decisive sea battle. The British wanted fixed patrol routes using destroyers and Italian dreadnoughts.

On the same day that war was declared, the Austrians had opened the offensive by bombarding numerous Italian cities along the Adriatic coast and the Tremiti islands while seaplanes bombed Venice. From their sheltered positions along the broken Adriatic coast, the Austrians' smaller, more mobile ships could attack Italy's open coastline at will. In the year before Italy entered the war, the French had suffered severe losses in the area. Lapeyrère's own flagship, the *Jean Bart*, had been torpedoed in late 1914, and the French armored cruiser *Léon Gambetta* had been sunk in April 1915 with 684 men on board.

The Duke, realizing that earlier attempts to lure the Austrians out of their safe harbors had been unsuccessful, felt that what was needed was a unified strategic offensive aimed at provoking a conclusive engagement. To this end, he planned a three-prong attack that would concentrate on the east coast of the Adriatic from Trieste to Cattaro (Kotor) and use the fast French destroyers. Italy's destroyers were unsuitable because they had been severely aged by the Libyan War and were in constant need of repair.

The first phase of the attack was a series of raids on the Dalmatian coast by the Allied fleet commanded by the Duke himself. These raids involved twelve French destroyers, twelve French torpedo boats, an array of minesweepers, seaplanes, and a seaplane carrier and occurred on June 1, 5, and 9.

The second phase of the operation began simultaneously and was designed to suppress Austrian activity along a 45-mile (72-kilometer) section of the lower Adriatic near the Straits of Otranto in order to protect the British supply lines in the Mediterranean. This operation was led by a reserve force of French destroyers and Italian light cruisers, operating under Admiral de Lapeyrère. A smaller, British contingent, commanded by Rear Admiral Cecil Thursby, of four British light cruisers and four British battleships was to assist in the blockade.

On June 9, Austrian submarines torpedoed and sank the British light cruiser *Dublin* and the Italian submarine *Medusa*. The Italians also lost a dirigible to ground fire.

Despite these losses, the Duke continued with his plan for the third phase of the attack: an invasion to capture the Dalmatian islands of Pelagosa and Lagosta, 28 and 36 miles (45 and 58 kilometers), respectively, from Gargano, a promontory extending east into the Adriatic and forming the spur on Italy's boot. Because of their proximity to Italy as well as the Dalmatian coast, these islands would serve as strategic bases from which the Allies could launch attacks on the Austrian naval base at Cattaro.

While the Duke was proceeding against Pelagosa, however, the Austrians bombarded Gargano. Believing the attack to be a diversionary tactic intended to draw the Italian fleet away from the more important port of Venice, Paolo Thaon di Revel, chief of staff of the Italian navy, commanded the Duke to detach a group of ships to the upper Adriatic for the protection of Venice. The Duke sent a division of battleships, four armored cruisers, and a squadron of destroyers under the command of Umberto Cagni, who was once again at his side. Cagni's fleet proceeded up the Adriatic, escorted by torpedo boats, and reached Venice safely on June 29. They would remain there throughout much of the war yet would be of little strategic value. The lumbering Italian ships were easy targets for the Austrian submarines. On July 7, the armored cruiser *Amalfi* was torpedoed and sunk 30 miles (48 kilometers) off Venice. Another severe blow came on July 19, when the flagship of the Adriatic fleet, the *Giuseppe Garibaldi*, was torpedoed and sunk off Cattaro while returning from a bombardment of Ragusa (Dubrovnik).

Meanwhile, on July 11, Italian forces had occupied Pelagosa. However, after the loss of the *Amalfi* and the *Giuseppe Garibaldi*, Thaon di Revel was reluctant to continue the action of the Duke's fleet by taking Lagosta. The Duke argued for a defensive occupation of Lagosta in order to defend Pelagosa from an enemy counterattack. While Thaon di Revel vacillated, the Austrians sank the sole Italian submarine defending Pelagosa and reoccupied the island.

Sir Herbert Richmond, the British liaison officer assigned to the Duke from May to December 1915, wrote in his diary that the Duke had demonstrated much ability and strength in his command. However, Richmond was shocked by the behavior of the Italian admiralty toward the Duke, who was continually hindered in action by the excessive caution and frustrating slowness of his superiors. It was Richmond's opinion that the occupation of Pelagosa had been interrupted too precipitously.

"They [the Italian admiralty] have by this admitted that the Austrians now have command of the sea in the Adriatic in spite of an inferior naval force," he wrote in his diary. "They had better sell their fleet, take up their organs and monkeys, for by Heaven, that seems more their profession than sea fighting."

After four months at war, Austria had sunk two of Italy's armored cruisers, one destroyer, two torpedo boats, three submarines, and two dirigibles. Italy had sunk only two Austrian submarines and three naval aircraft. Their smaller, faster fleet combined with their use of German-built submarines allowed the Austrians to sail the Adriatic with impunity.

As the losses mounted, the tension grew between the French and British commanders and the Italian admiralty. The French argued that the Italians were not accustomed to fleet work, avoided responsibility, and preferred to preserve their ships rather than risk losing them in battle. The British were particularly critical of Thaon di Revel's cautious strategy and the ineptness of Vice Admiral Leone Viale, who resigned as minister of the navy on September 24, 1915. On September 27, in the port of Brindisi, the powder magazine of the *Benedetto Brin*—proud dreadnought of the Italian fleet, which had fired the first shot at Tripoli—blew up. The great ship sank immediately, drowning the entire crew of 450 men.

On October 11, Thaon di Revel resigned as naval chief of staff, but the Italian parliament still needed a scapegoat. There was talk of sabotage, of negligence in surveillance on the part of the Secret Service. Although the Duke could not be blamed for the sinking of the *Benedetto Brin*, nevertheless, because of his position as commander in chief of the Allied navy, he was held accountable for the incident and the great loss.

Among the Allied officers, however, the Duke's performance as commander in chief remained beyond reproach. Admiral Mark Kerr, commander of the British Adriatic squadron, wrote in his diary that the Duke was a fine officer, both gallant and charming. British and French officers serving under the Duke affirmed that he did everything in his power to make things work smoothly among the Allies. According to one British officer, "He, unlike his superiors, would have gladly served under the French or British if by doing so he could have helped win a battle."

Sickened by the inefficiencies of the Italian ministry, Richmond requested to be relieved of his assignment, entering in his diary: "The Italian commander in chief has been the best man in his way that I have come across. He has listened and tried to do things, has adopted suggestions where he could, but has been blocked by this stupid staff at Rome in all important matters."

Unaware of the political maneuvering in Rome, the Duke was busy carrying out a military operation that would go down in history as a great humanitarian rescue mission.

In the summer of 1915, Serbian forces had successfully held their positions against superior German and Austrian forces along the Danube. However, in early September, when Bulgaria surrendered and proceeded to fight on the side of Austria, the Serbs were forced to retreat. On October 9, when the Austrians occupied the Serbian capital of Belgrade, nothing was left to the Serbs but full flight.

Throughout the winter, a half million Serbian refugees, soldiers and civilians alike, fled across the barren and rocky mountains with a single hope: to reach the coast. They were desperate—without food, without shelter to protect them from the cold, forced to drink water out of puddles to quench their thirst. To famine and privation was added a cholera epidemic. Less than half of the refugees reached the coast. There, salvation depended on the Allies, but the three Anglo-French divisions at Salonika made no move to help.

It was Italy that came to the refugees' aid. The minister of foreign affairs, Baron Sidney Sonnino, made a sorrowful speech before Parliament, saying, "Italy cannot remain insensible to the anguished call that comes across the Adriatic," and the Duke turned all his powers to bear on organizing a rescue mission.

His plan was to organize Italy's ailing destroyers and a collection of old cruisers to bring supplies from Brindisi across the Adriatic to San Giovanni di Medua in northern Albania. From there the supplies would be transported overland along Montenegro's Bojana River. On the return voyage, the vessels would carry survivors back to Italy.

The plan immediately raised opposition from the French, who wanted to use their large cruisers in the operation. The Duke objected on the grounds that the Albanian ports could not protect large steamers; in addition, shallow waters and poor docking facilities would prevent larger ships from unloading. He also felt that smaller ships would more easily avoid enemy detection and wanted to prevent the tremendous loss of life that would occur if a single large ship were to be sunk. In the face of unrelenting French criticism, a compromise was finally reached in which Great Britain would provide the supplies, Italy the ships and crews, and France a small protection unit of destroyers and cruisers.

Acting under the aegis of the Serbian Relief Committee, a coalition of British, French, and Italian relief efforts, the Duke began the rescue operation on December 12, 1915. His first charge was to equip the Italian ports, particularly their hospitals, with supplies and to arrange housing for a massive number of refugees. Winning the support of the Italian public in this effort was not easy when many thousands of Italians were dying in the trenches and the influx of foreign refugees would only add to the general hardship and famine, but in the end, generosity prevailed.

As soon as the Allied vessels began sailing to Albania with supplies, however, Austria sent its fastest ships and submarines to disrupt the mission, bombarding Italian ports and attacking the Allied contingent with torpedo boats and submarines. As the Duke had predicted, the largest ships were the first to be targeted: a single Austrian submarine succeeded in sinking five Allied steamers in a single day.

Over a period of four months, sailing yachts, coastal ships, British net drifters, and old steamers made more than two hundred trips across the dangerous Adriatic until the last refugee had been safely deposited on Italian soil. On January 22, 1916, the evacuation came to an end.

The losses were great: Austrian torpedoes had found their mark on many of the rescue ships, drowning hundreds of Italian, British, and French sailors and more than 60,000 Serbians. Italy lost six steamers, and France two of its ships. Brought to safety were 160,985 Serbians; 10,133 horses; 68 mortars; and 30,000 tons of military equipment.

Despite the success of the rescue operation and the enormous pride it aroused throughout Italy, criticism of the naval war effort focused once again on the Duke. In December 1916, French vice admiral Gauchet replaced Lapeyrère as commander of the Second Allied Fleet and refused to serve under an Italian. The Italian Ministry of the Navy similarly deemed it unthinkable to serve under the French in the Adriatic. After a stormy debate among the Allies in London, King Vittorio Emanuele III agreed that the command of the joint naval forces would be transferred to a French admiral provided the French would commit their entire fleet to the Adriatic.

In late January of 1917, King Vittorio Emanuele III reappointed Thaon di Revel to the position of chief of staff of the navy. In addition, he made him Commander of the Mobilized Naval Force, a position that in effect replaced that of the Duke. When Thaon di Revel offered the Duke the position of inspector general of the navy, reporting to him, Luigi di Savoia declined and gave his resignation. On February 3, the announcement of Thaon di Revel's appointment was made in Rome, along with that of the Duke's resignation "for reasons of ill health." In a move intended to sweep the ranks clean of the Duke's supporters, Cagni, then commander in chief at Brindisi, was demoted to a much smaller post at the maritime prefect at La Spezia.

The Duke's departure from command provoked an uproar among the Allies who had stood by the Duke's side in the years of battle in the Adriatic. The French called the king's decision to replace the Duke a "disgrace." The British admiral Mark Kerr stated that if the Duke's "shelving" had occurred in peacetime, he and his officers would have handed in their resignations. In a gesture of support, all the Allied officers accompanied the Duke to the train station at Taranto to say goodbye. Luigi di Savoia, touched but impassive, did not reveal by word or by gesture what lay in his soul.

Under the new French commander in chief, the Austrian incursions along the Italian coast were halted, but the French were never able to force a decisive showdown. Over the next few months, the Allied fleet would lose three more battleships, eight destroyers, and a score of submarines, torpedo boats, and other craft.

Now a civilian in a time of war, the Duke's life no longer belonged to his country. He asked the king for permission to enlist in the infantry to fight at the front, but his request was denied. Soldiers were dying by the hundreds of thousands on the northern front, and it was more useful to keep him alive as a national hero.

The Duke passed the last year of the war as a special aide to the king, often appearing at events aimed at boosting public morale. For the first time in nearly forty years he faced life without the deck of a ship under his feet.

Chapter Nine

℃

The Village
A Noble Experiment

ITALY HAD GAMBLED ON QUICK VICTORY WHEN IT FINALLY ENTERED THE war, but when the conflict finally ended in November 1918, the country was worse off than when it began. The war had cost Italy more than a million lives. Financially, it had drained the nation of 148 billion lire: double the general expenses of the state in the fifty-two years between 1861 and 1913. More than 4 million veterans returned home from the front to find their country in ruins. They had survived war only to face unemployment and starvation. Soon discontent and rebellion infected the nation.

Benefiting from the turmoil was Benito Mussolini, a former socialist and journalist who saw a path to political power through manipulating both the wealthy and the underprivileged. Mussolini ignited nationalist feelings by promising his supporters that Italy would stake its rightful claim to the Adriatic territories of Dalmatia and Albania and would take its "place in the sun" among Africa's colonial powers.

On March 23, 1919, Mussolini formed the Fasci Italiani di Combattimento (Italian League of Combat) with the intention of recreating the Roman Empire by expanding Italy's territory through conquest. Soon after, street fighting broke out in cities across Italy between the Fascists and members of the labor unions, Socialists, and anyone else who opposed them. The police refused to protect Mussolini's adversaries, and many were brutally beaten or murdered by his black-shirted mobs.

On October 28, 1922, Mussolini marched on Rome and took control of the government. In a rapid succession of events, he deprived Parliament of its authority and assumed dictatorial powers. The king had witnessed Mussolini's rise to power without opposition. One of the reasons given by historians for Vittorio Emanuele III's passivity was Mussolini's threat to depose him in favor of his cousin Emanuele Filiberto, the Duke of Aosta. The latter had made no secret of his sympathy for the Fascist cause, and the hero of the Third Army would have been a welcome replacement for the unpopular Vittorio Emanuele.

Unlike his brother Emanuele Filiberto, the Duke had always stayed on the margins of politics. He did not openly oppose Fascism, but neither did he approve of Mussolini's policies. Furthermore, he strongly disliked the coarseness and arrogance of the men who formed the Fascist government. For their part, while the Fascisti honored the Duke for his achievements, they stopped short of claiming him as a Fascist hero.

In 1924, the Duke was appointed Senatore del Regno ("Senator of the Realm"). The role was strictly nominal in a senate stripped of its powers, and the Duke rarely attended sessions. It was becoming less and less important to him to participate in the affairs of his country, for since 1918 he had been involved in creating a new life for himself in Africa.

The idea of creating an agricultural enterprise in Somaliland had been on the Duke's mind for years and had gained strength after he left the navy, especially during his time of forced inactivity as the war had raged about him. Since 1902, Vittorio Sella had been deeply involved in an agricultural enterprise his family had developed on reclaimed land in Sardinia, and he had often spoken about the business to the Duke on their expeditions to the Ruwenzori and the Karakoram as well as in numerous letters. Sella described himself as "a passionate farmer," and it is easy to see how the challenge of reclaiming land and setting up a flourishing agricultural business would have appealed to his pioneering spirit—and to that of the Duke as well.

Between the fall of 1918 and the spring of 1919, Luigi di Savoia made an exploratory trip to Benadir, the easternmost region of Somaliland, with his master at arms, Commander Radicati. He traveled the length and breadth of the country, trying to determine—in his thoroughly scientific manner—why other such experimental farms had failed.[20] Finally, discarding the valley of

the Juba River as being only partly within territory controlled by Italy, he focused his search in the region traversed by the Webi-Shebelle, a river parallel-
ing the coast through much of Italian Somaliland.

In October 1919, the Duke made a second trip to Somaliland to explore
the land bordering the Webi-Shebelle and to make definitive plans for the
farm. He arrived at Mogadishu on November 6, accompanied by Commander Francesco Bertonelli and a team of experts: agricultural and animal
adviser Giuseppe Scassellati Sforzolini, engineer Pier Gastone Agostinelli,
topographer Corrado Bellandi, cotton expert Guido Rossi, and technicians
Basilio Papa, Francesco Boero, and Alfredo Mercenaro. Also along was the
Duke's twenty-two-year-old nephew Amedeo, the son of Emanuele
Filiberto.

The team confirmed the feasibility of the project, and the Duke located
a possible site near the village of Giohàr (now Johar), some 80 miles (129
kilometers) northeast of Mogadishu. It was an area of woodland and
swamps, inhabited by snakes, leopards, and hyenas and infested with tsetse
flies, but it had several favorable characteristics. First of all, the land was
reasonably flat, with a slight inclination that would allow the building of an
irrigation network extending 5 miles (8 kilometers) on either side of the
Webi-Shebelle; the Duke had visited the region during different seasons and
found that the river could sustain such an irrigation system even during the
driest periods. The land was fertile but uninhabited, traveled mostly by
herdsmen and nomad farmers, who might be attracted to settling down
more permanently if they were given the opportunity to do so.

The Duke returned to Italy with all the information needed to perfect
the project and to raise the funds necessary for its realization. He also
counted on financing an expedition to follow the course of the Webi-
Shebelle to its sources in Ethiopia. However, once he drew up a financial
projection, he saw that the amount needed was enormous and that not many
investors would be anxious to give money to an enterprise that would take
years to show a profit. However, the Duke was not one to let himself be dis-
couraged, and he proceeded with the elaboration of the plan in all its details.

He decided to create a company, the Società Agricola Italo-Somala
(S.A.I.S.), that would lease the land and hire local labor in exchange for
lodging, a share of the harvest, and a salary. This formula was similar to the
crop sharing (*mezzadria*) that he had observed in Tuscany, where the Aostas

owned property, and which functioned profitably in the northern part of Italy. In contrast, the farms of southern Italy consisted of large estates owned by members of the aristocracy and cultivated by day laborers working for minimum wages, a system that only perpetuated the poverty of the peasants.

In the Duke's plans for his farm in Somaliland, each family of workers would be given a house and about one hectare of reclaimed and irrigated land. Half of the land would be cultivated with maize, durra, vegetables, and legumes, a portion of which would be retained by the family for its own use. The other half of the land would be reserved for commercial crops, such as cotton and sesame, and the harvest would be allotted to the S.A.I.S. to sell or to process in the factories to be constructed on the farm.

The S.A.I.S. would provide land, housing, and wells for drinking water, as well as work animals such as oxen and mules. It would furnish farming tools and seeds, and help the settlers with low-interest loans and crop bonuses. The farmers and their families could earn additional income by working in fields managed directly by the S.A.I.S. for the production of sugar cane, kapok, castor-oil seed, and other crops destined for Italian industries.

The Duke's plans were worked out down to the smallest detail and included an analysis of all the preliminary construction, such as clearing the forest and building dikes and irrigation networks, as well as houses, stables, storehouses, and service buildings.

The plan also provided for a transportation system. In summer, the roads leading to the farm site were often covered with sand, and in the rainy season, they were impassable with mud. The Duke therefore proposed building a branch railroad that would link the farm to the main railroad line between Mogadishu and Lugh. He also planned to exploit the river. The Webi-Shebelle had never been considered navigable, but the Duke—on the basis of numerous surveys made during his exploratory trips—believed it would be feasible to use barges to transport the sand and stones needed for construction from nearby quarries.

A substantial part of the foreseen expense was allotted for acquiring machinery, equipment, and motor vehicles.

His plan completed, the Duke now had to find investors who would become partners in his company. Filled with fervor, he traveled incessantly from Milan to Genoa, to Turin, to Venice, to Rome, meeting with industrialists, bankers, and possible investors of every kind. He used his name and earlier success as a brilliant speaker to hold meetings and give lectures on the farm project. His reputation as an explorer and admiral would have been of little use, however, without the passion and zeal with which he spoke of his dream.

In his lectures he began to sound like a missionary, stating that the precarious level of life of the Somali people was not due "to the poverty of the biological environment or to unsurmountable hindrances" but was the result "of various combined geographical, historical, and political factors, of age-old isolation, of the social structure." He was convinced that by improving the social structure and offering possibilities of work, the men could be redeemed from their paralyzing fatalism and resignation and could open themselves to a life of hope and trust.

In November 1920, the S.A.I.S. was registered at the Chamber of Commerce of Milan with a total investment of 24 million lire. Within four years, investment in the company would increase to 35 million lire. The shareholders consisted of bankers, industrialists, and ordinary citizens, including Vittorio Sella, his brothers, and his cousins. The Duke himself contributed 2 million lire and was designated president and general director of the company.

One of the Duke's most loyal financial supporters in the years to come would be Katherine Elkins. After the end of their romantic relationship in 1913, they had continued to keep in contact through correspondence. Now married and living in Middleburg, Virginia, Katherine had inherited a large portion of her father's $30 million railroad and mining estate. She spent her time traveling between Paris and America and also ran a fashionable horse-breeding farm, raising champion show horses. She regularly sent money and supplies—including the latest in modern medical, road building, and railroad equipment—either anonymously or under a false name to the Duke's farm in Somaliland. The extent of her contributions appears to have contributed to her divorce from Billy Hitt in 1921.

Once the S.A.I.S was founded, the Duke received dispensations from the Italian Ministry of Colonies that allowed him to obtain at low cost various items salvaged from the war—including motor vehicles, narrow-gauge Décauville railway tracks, and even a captured tugboat—as well as tax exemptions, customs waivers, and permission to hire labor in Somaliland. He also secured financing to build a railway connection between Mogadishu and the farm.

In the course of his exploratory trips, the Duke had learned the three main dialects of Somaliland, which now proved useful to him in land negotiations with the chiefs of the Scindle tribes. An agreement was made in which the S.A.I.S. would lease 25,000 hectares of land: 16,000 on the left bank of the Webi-Shebelle—including the villages of Giohàr Eilo, Balguri, Bajahao, Racheilo Omar Gudle—and 9,000 hectares on the right bank, with the villages of Colundi, Burei, Moico, and Nucai. Other villages of herdsmen and farmers living farther from the river were added to the settlement, whose population now totaled 2,374. The colony also included some 870 hectares of land that were already being cultivated and a forest that would provide timber for all the construction, as well as fuel for the steam engines and the furnaces used in producing bricks and tiles.

The first thing the Duke did was build a dam, using local workers, that would divert the river to feed a network of irrigation canals. The land destined for cultivation then had to be deforested and the marshes drained. The bush was so dense it could only be cut by hand, but the Somalis turned out to be skilled woodsmen. The huge termite hills that rose in ochre spires from the newly cleared land were demolished with explosives, and the uneven ground was leveled with tractors. The rough tracks leading to the farm were transformed into proper roads that could accommodate not only camel caravans but also trucks heavily loaded with cement, wood, and food supplies.

The middle branch of the Webi-Shebelle had to be drained, cleaned, and dredged for 259 miles (416 kilometers) so that barges could navigate from Afgoi to Bulo-Burti, where the stone quarries were located. The Duke himself supervised the design of special tow boats, which were built in Castellammare near Naples, then dismantled, transported to Somaliland, and reassembled at Afgoi. Over the next five years, these barges would carry more than 30,000 tons of construction material to the new settlement, which had been christened Villaggio Duca degli Abruzzi (Duke of the Abruzzi Village) by the governor of Italian Somaliland, when he visited the site in 1921.

The agreement with the tribal chiefs had leased the reclaimed lands to the S.A.I.S. for ninety years, at the end of which time, the property would return to the ownership of the local population. In addition, the S.A.I.S. was allowed to purchase land on which to build houses, churches, hospitals, and schools. Another clause of the agreement bound the chiefs to furnish workers to the S.A.I.S. The principal problem with previous colonial farms had been, above all, the lack of manual labor, for the nomadic population was reluctant to remain in one place. If they did settle for a time, they eventually returned to their life as migrant herdsmen. The Scindle people, who inhabited the agricultural area along the river, were also reluctant to leave their villages and their tribal customs.

The Duke had visited and studied earlier settlements and was convinced that the solution to the problem was to construct dwellings that would allow the workers to organize their life exactly as in their home villages. He therefore had a mosque and a bazaar constructed at the same time as the houses were built, and the settlement was structured as a collection of many smaller villages to allow family and tribal units to be grouped together.

The Duke also believed that the success of his enterprise depended on guaranteeing maximum commitment from the Italian side if he wanted to obtain maximum cooperation from the local workers. The agreement between the S.A.I.S. and the Somali chiefs was therefore not a simple private contract but had decidedly political connotations. The Duke's intuition was on the mark and gained him the goodwill of the local populations, whose participation was crucial for the success of his enterprise.

No sooner had the construction work started than men from all the neighboring villages began to arrive, urged by the chiefs who had signed the agreement with S.A.I.S. and attracted by the promise of good wages. Soon, the colony resounded with different dialects amid the construction of houses, stables, storehouses, and vehicle sheds. The company did not want a shantytown and therefore permitted no temporary shelters. All buildings had to be built solidly and to last.

A power plant was constructed to supply electricity to the administrators' houses and the offices, as well as to the factories, which included oil, cereal, and cotton mills; water distillation and refrigeration plants; a machine shop; and a dairy. A large sugar refinery was added later.

By 1926, Duke of the Abruzzi Village consisted of sixteen smaller villages housing three thousand Somalis and two hundred Italians. A hospital had been constructed, complete with a modern surgery. There were schools, and next to the mosque, a Catholic church dedicated to Our Lady of Consolation, the traditional protectress of the House of Savoy. There were even shops and a movie theater. In addition, the Duke had founded a laboratory for agronomy research in order to continually improve the agricultural methods of the farm. More than 52 miles (84 kilometers) of newly built roads connected the colony's villages, along with a 22-mile (35-kilometer) narrow-gauge railroad and miles and miles of telephone lines.

At the beginning, things were not easy. It took time before the Somalis became used to living at the Village, and epidemics of illness caused labor shortages at critical times in the production process. In the Duke's correspondence with Sella he mentions financial difficulties—then suddenly all such allusions ended. Probably the help of Katherine Elkins at some point resolved the crisis.

The Duke served as president of the S.A.I.S. and was personally in charge of conducting the business until the end of his life. He spent several months a year at the Village, which became his primary preoccupation and his dearest achievement, but returned to Italy often to visit family and friends and to attend to administrative details of the company, which was headquartered there.

The Duke's family and friends did not come to see him in Somaliland, except for his sister-in-law, Hélène, a passionate traveler who had always been devoted to him. Motherless from an early age, Luigi di Savoia responded warmly to Hélène's affection. If his aunt Margherita had influenced him in his love of mountains, his sister-in-law was certainly the relative with whom he most shared his love of Africa.

Even Sella, now in his late sixties, never visited the Duke at the Village—the sea voyage would have taken too much time, and Sella was too occupied with his family business and his photography to be able to leave them for long. The two men wrote often, however, and the Duke visited with Sella each time he returned to Italy. Like most farmers, they discussed the problems of reclaiming the land and experimenting with crops.

The Duke was growing older, and his health was beginning to deteriorate. He had caught malaria in 1919, on his second exploratory trip to Somaliland. Although he recovered, at that time the only treatment for malaria was quinine, and no recovery was really definitive.

And yet, notwithstanding the infirmities of age and the cares of the Village, the Duke had not set aside his adventurous past. For a long time he had been thinking of exploring the river that sustained the Village. He knew time was passing quickly, and before it was too late he wanted to undertake one last expedition.

Chapter Ten

℣

Webi-Shebelle
The Last Expedition

Ever since he had begun to plan his agricultural village, the Duke had wanted to explore the Webi-Shebelle and had made requests for financing to both the Ministry of the Colonies and the Italian Geographic Society. Despite the disastrous state of its finances, the government considered the project useful to Italy's colonial aspirations and gave its approval.

On February 23, 1918—while Italy was still at war—the minister of the colonies presented his report on the project to the Chamber of Deputies, and on November 23, 1918—scarcely three weeks after the war had ended—the vice president of the Italian Geographic Society announced that, in conjunction with the Ministry of the Colonies and with the patronage of the king, the society was preparing an expedition to explore the middle and upper courses of the Webi-Shebelle.

Because the lower course of the river lay entirely within the territory of Italian Somaliland, the expedition would have commercial and political ramifications in addition to its purely geographical value. The Ministry of the Colonies was interested chiefly in the effects the exploration of the river would have on the development of farming settlements in Somaliland. For the Geographic Society, the journey would complete the work initiated by another Italian explorer, Vittorio Bottego, who had led two previous expeditions to investigate the Juba and Omo Rivers.

Bottego had arrived in Eritrea as an army officer in 1887 and was the

first European to travel the coast from Mesewa to Aseb. In 1892, he organized an expedition to explore the Juba River along its main branch, which
he called the Doria Channel. In the course of this journey, he also completed a partial reconnaissance of the Webi-Shebelle. His more important
exploration, however, was of the Omo River, which between 1895 and 1897
he traced from Lugh to Lake Margherita, and then as far as Lake Rodolfo
(now Lake Turkana). On his return journey, he was ambushed by native
warriors and killed.

The Shebelle, or Sciaveli, River had been known since ancient times.
According to a recurring legend in the stories of Arabian geographers, the
Somalian territory was crossed by a large river that flowed into the Indian
Ocean and which was called the Second Nile or the Somali Nile. Apart
from the legend, however, there was no evidence of the existence of the
river because the coast of Somaliland is barred by a long chain of dunes
blocking any river from emptying into the ocean.

In 1844, William Christopher, a British army officer, received permission from the Sultan of Gheledi to explore the territory behind the dunes.
What Christopher found was a great river that ran parallel to the coast. It
was called Webi, the common name for "river" in that region. Christopher
followed its course for some 124 miles (200 kilometers) and became convinced that the river could not possibly flow into the ocean across the
dunes, which offered no opening.

Three years later, a French officer named Guillain visited the Webi at
Gheledi, near Mogadishu, where he gathered information from local people
about the river and its sources, which were supposedly in the mountainous
regions inhabited by the Galla Arussi, south of Addis Ababa in Ethiopia.
Apparently the river flowed east, collecting water from tributaries descending from the high plains of Harrar, and then curved south into the flatlands
behind the dunes.

There were other explorations as well, including two in Ethiopia. In
1886, the Italian Leopoldo Traversi, who was part of a permanent military
mission in the court of the Abyssinian king Menelik at Entotto, accompanied a military expedition of Menelik against the Galla Arussi in the mountains south of Addis Ababa and had the chance to observe several different
rivers. These rivers were, however, branches of the same river, which the local inhabitants called Wabi (a variation of Webi), or Wabi-Webi-Shebelle,

"River of the Leopards." In the same year, Vincenzo Ragazzi, another Italian serving with Traversi, followed Menelik's army in the conquest of Harrar, and wrote an account of his traverse of the vast region in which the sources of the Wabi-Webi are found.

Other expeditions in succeeding years examined the middle course of the Shebelle. Guillain had already reported the existence of another large river that traversed the southern territory of Somaliland and flowed into the Indian Ocean. This was the Juba, later explored by Bottego.

It took many years and several explorations to solve the mystery of the mythical Second Nile. It was eventually determined that there were two different rivers and that the Webi-Shebelle, after its long course in a marshy band parallel to the coast, emptied into the Juba, which, in turn, was fed by the steep sloping watershed to the south of the Webi-Shebelle. The lower courses of the river had been mapped by these expeditions, and it remained to explore the upper reaches of the river and to identify its sources, which lay somewhere in Ethiopia.

By 1928, when the Duke was ready to mount his expedition, Italy had already had a long and rocky colonial history in Ethiopia, and political negotiations would be necessary for the Duke to explore in Ethiopian territory. In 1882 and 1885, Italy had acquired the Eritrean seaports of Aseb and Mesewa, and in 1889, when King Menelik became emperor of Ethiopia after conquering and annexing most of the territories adjacent to his small kingdom, he had signed a treaty of cooperation with Italy—the Treaty of Ucciali—which made Ethiopia an Italian protectorate. Menelik, however, had abrogated the treaty in 1893 and in 1896 had decisively defeated the Italian armies at Adwa, establishing Ethiopia's independence.

In 1913 Menelik died, and in 1916 the Scioa chiefs put Menelik's daughter Zaudità on the throne under the regency of Ras (chief) Tafari Maconnèn. In 1928, Tafari Maconnèn, who had, in fact, been the true sovereign of Ethiopia since the beginning of his regency, assumed power and declared himself Plenipotentiary Vicar of the Empire and Emperor of Ethiopia. Upon Zaudità's death in 1930, he ascended the throne as Emperor of Emperors, taking the name Haile Selassie I.

Even before Maconnèn assumed power in 1928, he had sought to develop friendly relations with Italy, to the point of making an official visit to the king in Rome. In 1927, the Duke was named ambassador to Ethiopia and was charged with reciprocating Tafari Maconnèn's visit. He took the occasion to request the regent's permission for the Webi-Shebelle expedition and received not only authorization, but the promise of assistance and an armed escort.

On October 1, 1928, the expedition sailed from Italy to Djibouti and from there proceeded to Addis Ababa by train. They remained for some time in the capital, participating in celebrations organized by Tafari Maconnèn in their honor, and on October 26 finally departed by train for Hadama, where their exploration would begin on foot, at 6,643 feet (1,720 meters) above sea level.

The expedition had received financial backing in the amount of 50,000 lire from the Italian Geographic Society and another 300,000 lire from the Ministry of the Colonies. As he had so often done before, the Duke had assembled a team whose various skills would help him with the scientific investigations. This core group included seven men: Enrico Cerulli, attaché to the Italian legation in Addis Ababa and an expert in languages, particularly the Abyssinian and Somali dialects, who would be responsible for anthropological research and relations with the Abyssinian chiefs; Edoardo Tischer, chief of mechanical and industrial services at S.A.I.S., charged with organizing the caravans and collecting ore samples; navy surgeon Cosimo Basile, who would act as expedition doctor and also collect botanical and zoological samples; Captain Fabrizio Palazzolo and Lieutenant Giovanni Braca, both topographers from the Military Geographic Institute, charged with making topographic and astronomical measurements and relief maps; Edmondo Angeli, navy radiotelegraph operator, who would be responsible for telegraphic communication as well for making photographic and cinemagraphic records of the expedition; and, finally, Orazio Pavanello, chief of the S.A.I.S. topographical survey office, who would be in charge of meteorological observations and also aid the Duke in his astronomical measurements.

This was a military expedition, and for the first time the Duke was not surrounded by his dear companions or assisted by his faithful alpine guides. Petigax had died two years earlier, and Cagni, now in his mid-sixties, had been retired for some time. Also missing were De Filippi and Sella, who was now nearly seventy. The fifty-five-year old Duke shared his tent with thirty-year-old Lieutenant Braca, the youngest man on the expedition. Braca was so in awe of his royal tentmate that he removed the tent stakes on his side of the tent so he could slip quietly into bed by crawling under the tent wall after the Duke was asleep without disturbing him. He also tied a string around his wrist, with the loose end outside the tent. His attendant would wake him up early in the morning by jerking on the string, and Braca would make his exit in the same way before the Duke awakened. One day, the Duke asked him, "How is it that I never see you coming into the tent or leaving it? Where do you sleep?" It is said that Braca blushed with embarrassment but did not reveal his secret.

The rest of the expedition was composed of numerous porters, selected from Eritrean Muslims to avoid any problems with the Islamic populations they would encounter in the highlands. Rather than going by train to Hadama, the porters instead climbed the entire way from their villages with the camels and mules hired by Tischer to transport the provisions and other supplies.

It took two days to organize the caravan, which finally set out on October 28, 1928, escorted by a detachment of machine-gunners from the emperor's personal army, another of Eritrean riflemen, and a squadron of Galla warriors on horseback. In all, there were more than a hundred armed men, under the orders of the Ethiopian liaison officer Baianè, who had the privilege of "presenting himself early in the morning at the camp of the white men to give the order for the caravan to depart."

After having studied the reports of previous explorers, the Duke had decided to explore the mountain range that separated the basin of the Webi-Shebelle from the Awash River. The region had been recently conquered by Menelik and was inhabited by diverse ethnic groups: Galla, Arussi, Balis, Somalis, and Harrarines. Each was administered by a governor who headed a complicated political hierarchy. As had happened on the Ruwenzori expedition, each time the caravan entered a new ethnic region, they were greeted by a crowd of local authorities who, with great pomp and ceremony, escorted them to the border of the territory, where they were handed over to the authorities of the next region, who welcomed them again in the same lavish manner. This armed and motley crowd, added to the escort furnished by the emperor, made the expedition look more like a barbarian army on the march than a European scientific expedition. The logistical complications created by such a throng were enormous, and it took all the experience of a navy commander to succeed in disentangling them. What a difference from the solitude and purity of the Arctic and the highest mountains of the world!

The object of the exploration of this territory was to locate the sources of the Webi-Shebelle and then to follow the course of the river into Somaliland. The explorers made their way toward the highlands of the Arussi, proceeding between Mount Cilalo and Lake Zwai. The land was fertile and cultivated up to 8,202 feet (2,500 meters). Above, the highlands extended in a vast flat savanna, dominated by the cones of Zuquala and other minor mountains.

The expedition continued climbing, reaching the Carra Col at 10,335 feet (3,150 meters), then crossing a range of 13,000-foot (4,000-meter) mountains, and finally arriving at the upper basin of the Webi-Shebelle, called the Ghedeb—an immense grassy plateau about 8,500 feet (2,600 meters) in elevation, carved by numerous rivers that had cut deep canyons into the tableland. Here, the caravan halted at Malca Daddecià ("Glade of the Acacias"), named for the few large acacias that grew near the river, the only trees the men had glimpsed in many days of walking. The party remained at the glade a few days to rest, and to test an inflatable boat that would help them transport supplies across the numerous river fords to come. They also carried out topographic and scientific surveys.

While at the glade, the expedition was visited by herders and inhabitants of villages that the men had not even noticed, and from their words and gestures the Duke was able to understand that the source of the Webi— here called the Wabi—was not far away. It was difficult to interpret the rather vague and sometimes conflicting directions of the locals, and even more difficult to decide which direction to take on the deeply cut terrain, but the Duke's intuition put them on the right path.

After days of marching single-file along rivers set deep in narrow gorges, the expedition arrived at a beautiful forest of junipers. From here, a narrow trail ascended to a marshy highland called Hoghisò or Hoghesò, which formed the border between the lands of the Arussi and those of the Sidamo.

On November 12, during a heavy rain, the Duke was leading a small group detached from the main body of the expedition, which had become lost in the forest of junipers, when suddenly they found themselves before an enclosure built of bamboo canes. A passing herder told them that this was a sacred site, and the Duke realized that they had reached the source of the Webi-Shebelle. Kneeling down, he gathered the water in his cupped hands and raised them in a sacramental gesture.

The area, however, was not suitable for a camp, and the Duke went to look for a place that was drier and more sheltered from the wind. He had gone off a little ways when he became aware that he had lost a ring that he usually kept in a small pocket of his jacket. It had perhaps fallen out when he had leaned over the waters of the source. Alarmed, he turned back and began to search for it, asking everyone to help him, but in vain. It was raining, the rest of the caravan arrived, and the ring had not been found. The Duke abandoned the search and gave orders to set up the tents.

Later, alone in the tent with Braca, the Duke broke down. According to Braca—now a retired general in his nineties—the Duke said that the ring had been given to him by the only woman he had ever loved. In obedience to his cousin the king, who had appealed to the Duke's sense of duty but in reality was acting out of spite, he had not married her. At this point, the Duke was shaking with emotion and anger, and the startled Braca could not believe his ears. The Duke continued, saying that he would have given everything, title and career, to marry this woman even against the opposition of the king, but that he did not possess a personal fortune and could never have agreed to let himself be maintained by a wealthy woman.

The Duke's observations established the location of the source of the Webi-Shebelle at 6°50'17" north latitude and 38°42'39" east longitude. Reunited in the camp, the men began preparations to map the river down the entirety of its course.

That day, they received a visit from a white man, the only white man they would encounter on their entire journey from Hadama in Ethiopia to Sul Sul in Somaliland. The visitor was a French Catholic priest, who had lived so long on shores of Lake Zwai that he had forgotten how many years he had been in Africa. The Duke felt a profound kinship for this man, one of the many nameless missionaries who dedicated their lives to a continent despoiled and plundered by their European brothers. The priest told them he had heard of the expedition from the local people and had set out on his mule to meet them. He had been traveling for several days and had brought as a gift some fruit and a few vegetables. Delivering his presents, he departed the same day, to return to Zwai on the back of his mule.

Now the river began to divide, and the expedition separated into groups to explore the various branches. One party, scouting the territory to the west, discovered that the Juba also had its origins in the same savannas that gave birth to the Webi-Shebelle.

Despite frequent halts in their explorations due to the rain and various other obstacles, the expedition reunited to traverse the lowlands of Ambientù and forded the Weyib, a tributary of Juba, at its only possible crossing—a dangerous eddy some 92 feet (28 meters) wide and 13 feet (4 meters) deep. Thanks to their ability and a good deal of luck they gained the other side without incident and reached Birbisà, a village inhabited by poor peasants and one of the few settlements they had encountered along the entire journey.

Little by little they followed the river downstream, the temperature rising and the vegetation growing ever more luxuriant. The banks of the river were green with acacias, euphorbias, and wild olives. Always descending, the expedition arrived at Gore, where they met caravans of pilgrims bound for the tomb of Scheck Hussein, a Muslim holy man venerated in the entire world of Islam. The devotees came not only from the surrounding regions, but also from Arabia and far distant countries. The tomb itself was located in a small mosque taken care of by a Galla family, following a tradition dating back to the sixteenth century.

The expedition rested for nine days near Scheck Hussein's tomb, then took up their journey on rocky ground with scarce vegetation. The monotony of the barren landscape was interrupted by huge termite hills towering as high as 13 feet, and the roughness of the terrain made it difficult for the mules and camels to proceed. The camels originally brought from Addis Ababa had been replaced with others acquired at Scheck Hussein, but the change did not result in much advantage because the new camels were untamed and caused quite a few accidents that slowed down the progress of the caravan.

Once more the expedition had to divide, for the Webi-Shebelle was encased in a gorge with walls 1,300 feet high that the caravan could not descend. The Duke assigned some porters and a small escort to the two topographers so they could travel with greater autonomy, and they separated from the main group. The rest of the caravan proceeded slowly while the topographers made frequent side trips down to the river.

The banks of the river exhibited a wilder atmosphere than that of the highlands. The waters were infested with crocodiles, and at the site the topographers had selected for their camp, they found the fresh remains of two camels that had been devoured by lions. They met almost no one beyond a few infrequent nomads. Their work nevertheless was satisfying, and on December 27 they rejoined the caravan at Sauena. The rest of the expedition had celebrated Christmas two days earlier, at Miaua, in a beautiful forest rich with game.

On December 29, Pavanello and Braca again separated from the caravan to explore the tributaries of the river while the Duke and the main force proceeded along the stony ground covered with thorny brush until they reached the rocky valley of the Dare River. Although the river was dry, the banks were covered with beautiful doom palms that offered the tired men a cool respite from the harsh sun.

The caravan continued along the riverbed, following its twisting contours. They were now in Imi territory and were coming to the end of their long journey. On January 7, 1929, Ethiopian Christmas, the expedition reached the lowland plains, and the Duke called a stop to allow the Abyssinian men to celebrate the day.

Pavanello and Braca continued with their surveying and rejoined the group at Malca Dube with stories of terrifying adventures. They had found extraordinary numbers of wild animals at the water holes: lions devouring an antelope, vultures waiting for the remains of the kill, crocodiles in the middle of where they had put their tent. Braca and the Somali cook had been attacked by a leopard, and although Braca's wounds were light, the leopard's teeth had cut clean through two tendons of the cook's arm. Without a doctor, Pavanello and Braca did not know what to do. Seeing that it would take several days to get back to camp and that the dangling tendons were bleeding with great risk of infection, they decided to cut the tendons off and somehow closed the wound. The cook lost partial use of his arm, but his life had been saved.

Only 124 miles (200 kilometers) remained until the end of the journey. From Malca Dube on, the territory had already been explored and mapped, but it seemed a completely different country from what Bottego had described in his accounts. In Bottego's time, the banks of the rivers were populated with several small villages. Now there were only ruins, devastated by bands of

Abyssinian tribesmen who had joined the Ethiopian army as it fought its way down from the highlands and who had, in exchange for their service, been left free to ransack, burn, and destroy as they pleased. The fields lay abandoned, and the surviving villagers were hiding in the forest.

As soon as word of the caravan spread, crowds of the wounded and ill came out from their hiding places to seek the help of a physician—the "white doctor" that they knew always accompanied an expedition. For the remainder of the journey, Basile worked without rest to treat them.

Finally, on February 3, 1929, the caravan reached Mustahil, a village on the border of Italian Somaliland. Later, at Sul Sul, the Duke was greeted by the regent of the colony together with the officers and directors of the S.A.I.S., who had come from Abruzzi Village with trucks to carry the men and materials home.

Only the topographers stayed a few days longer to check their data, as they had found errors in the maps of their predecessors.

The Ethiopian escort accompanied the Duke's party to Mogadishu with many thanks and honors for their efforts. From there they continued the journey by sea to Djibouti and then by train to Addis Ababa.

The expedition had taken one hundred days, and the caravan had traveled a total of 870 miles (1,400 kilometers) in sixty-seven stages, each an average of 13 miles (21 kilometers). The objectives had been fulfilled: the source of the Webi-Shebelle had been located and its upper basin explored and mapped. As in the Duke's previous expeditions, precious data and materials had been collected: astronomical and geodetic measurements; meteorological and hydrographic data; important observations concerning tropical diseases; anthropological and ethnographic notes; and samples of rocks, plants, and animals.

But for the Duke of the Abruzzi this expedition was unlike the others he had conceived and directed. Rather than bringing him fame and fortune, it was barely noticed, being only one of many expeditions sponsored by European states anxious to develop their colonial possessions. For the Duke, who had dedicated ten years of his life to developing an agricultural enterprise in a land that he considered not just a colony but his second homeland, this last expedition represented an opportunity to follow once more his own dream of adventure and at the same time render a service to the country in which his Village had taken root.

It was a tragic irony of fate that the maps drawn as a result of the Duke's expedition opened the way to Mussolini's armies, which a few years later set about the conquest of Ethiopia in a cruel and bloody war. Fortunately, the Duke was spared this knowledge. When the war began in October 1935, he had been dead for more than two years.

Chapter Eleven

₡

Final
Resting Place

THE OFFICIAL REPORT OF THE WEBI-SHEBELLE EXPEDITION WAS PUBLISHED in 1932. As with all his previous expeditions, the Duke personally assembled the diaries and notes written by himself and by the other members of the expedition. And as usual, he entrusted Filippo De Filippi, even though he had not taken part in the expedition, with writing the narrative, which, however, appeared under the Duke's name.

The Duke was also a principal photographer on the expedition. He had borrowed Sella's Zeiss Ikon camera with the Z. Tessar lens and the airtight camera case Sella had used in the Ruwenzori and the Karakoram and had also helped to shoot a motion picture of the expedition, which was premiered in Rome at the Cinema Moderno in May 1929.

Following the expedition, the Duke returned to Abruzzi Village, where he continued to develop the various farm projects. He usually spent his summers in Italy, but in 1929 he returned earlier in order to give several lectures and to see his physicians. For several years he had suffered from diabetes, and during the Webi-Shebelle expedition he had been under the constant medical supervision of Doctor Basile. However, despite the strenuous long marches and survey operations, he had had no trouble except for one small incident. Momentarily alone in a dense forest, he had found a honeycomb in the hollow of a tree and could not resist the temptation to taste it. He ended up eating the entire comb and later that evening became very ill.

Basile could not understand what was wrong because the Duke was reluctant to confess his schoolboy mischief. When he finally told what he had done, Basile gave him a shot of insulin, and he recovered quickly.

During the winter of 1928–1929, he began to suffer other problems that made him decide he needed to consult with his doctors. He took advantage of the trip to spend a tranquil summer at Oropa, in the mountains near Biella, and also went to Courmayeur to attend a ceremony of the Società delle Guide, where he met with Sella to discuss a photo exhibit for a mountaineering museum being built in Courmayeur. Sella wrote in his journal that the Duke was once again restored to youth by the treatment of sun and water.

In autumn he returned to Somaliland, appearing to Sella to be "bright and cheerful" as he departed. He did not remain at the Village long, however, for his illness worsened, and he returned to Turin for an operation. Cancer of the prostate was discovered, a disease that would prove fatal. The operation, however, temporarily arrested the progress of the tumor, and the Duke was to enjoy three more years of activity, always in motion, traveling between Italy and Somaliland, always immersed in work, always ready to participate in every event at which his presence was requested.

He returned to Italy on sad occasions. In 1931, both his brother Emanuele Filiberto and his friend Umberto Cagni died. His aunt Margherita had died in 1926 at age seventy-five. Now there was almost no one in Italy with whom he had emotional ties. Joseph Petigax had also died in 1926, and the Duke had gone to Courmayeur to comfort the widow of the guide to whom he had been so greatly devoted. An entire world was disappearing. The Duke no longer ventured into the mountains except for short walks. He sent a postcard to Vittorio Sella, saying, "This is the maximum altitude I can manage."

Every time he was near Biella, he went to visit Sella and his family. The Duke had always been a passionate reader, particularly of scientific and travel books; now he became interested in contemporary literature and devoured book after book, which he loved to exchange and discuss with Sella's wife, Linda, and with the other women of the family.

In Somalia the Duke lived a quiet and secluded life in the small house he had had built in the heart of the Village. Living with him was a young Somali woman whose existence no one knew about until, in April 1987, the architect Aldo Audisio, director of the Museo Nationale della Montagna in

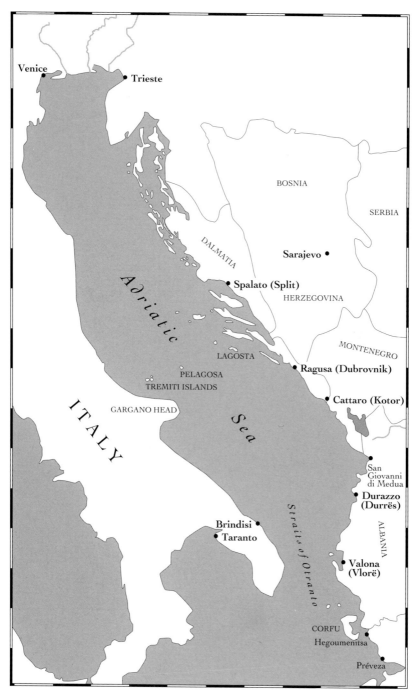

Venice

Trieste

BOSNIA

SERBIA

DALMATIA

Sarajevo

Spalato (Split)

HERZEGOVINA

Adriatic

MONTENEGRO

LAGOSTA

Ragusa (Dubrovnik)

PELAGOSA
TREMITI ISLANDS

Cattaro (Kotor)

GARGANO HEAD

Sea

ITALY

San
Giovanni
di Medua

Durazzo
(Durrës)

Brindisi
Taranto

Straits of Otranto

ALBANIA

Valona
(Vlorë)

CORFU
Hegoumenitsa

Préveza

24 *The Adriatic Sea at the time of World War I*

25 *The Duke in his admiral's uniform*

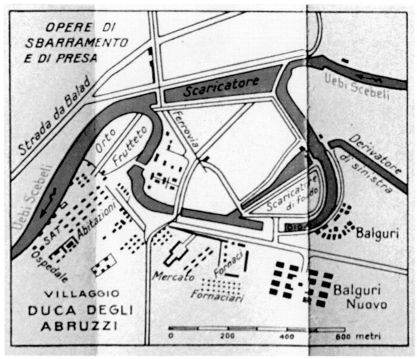

26 *Duke of the Abruzzi Village*

27 *Somali market near the Village*

28 *The Duke with a dead antelope*

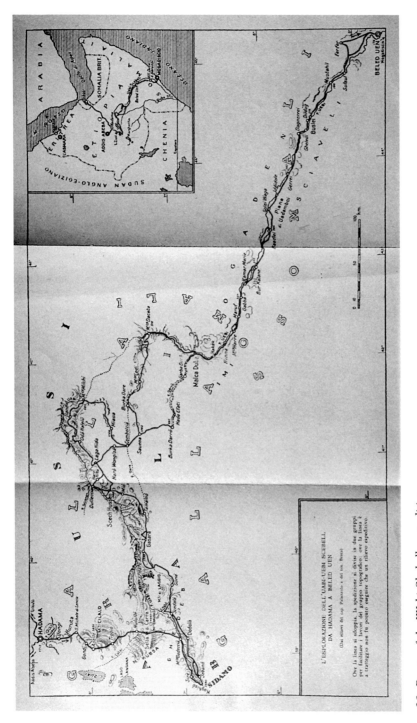

29 *Route of the Webi-Shebelle expedition*

30 *Camels crossing the Webi-Shebelle*

32 *The Duke being saluted on his arrival in Mogadishu* ➤

31 *The Duke is greeted in the Village after his return from the Webi-Shebelle expedition*

Al Principe diletto
Reduce glorioso dai
perigli del Polo la
Patria in lutto per
la recente sventura
tende affettuosa le
braccia.

W. Luigi di Savoia — W. Cagni —

A Guarneri - Milano - N. 4076

33 A postcard celebrating the Duke's exploits and displaying the signatures
of the Duke and Cagni

Turin (which is dedicated to the Duke of the Abruzzi) went to visit the Village. In the entrance hall of the Duke's home he noticed the bust of a woman, and deciphering the name incised in the base of the sculpture—Faduma Ali—he asked the caretaker who she was. The caretaker, son of the Duke's former steward, told him that she had been the lady of the house and the Duke's unofficial wife.

Ernesto Milanese, of the Faculty of Agronomy at the University of Florence, during a period of teaching agronomy in Afgoi also visited the Village and sought to learn something more about Faduma Ali. Some of the older villagers remembered her, or had heard tell of her. They related that she came from Migiurtinia, a coastal region of Somaliland famous for its coconuts, its dates—and its beautiful women. She was said to be of noble birth and highly educated. The villagers knew her as Regina ("Queen"), an Italian name common among Somali women. The bust in the hallway had been commissioned by the Duke and had been placed by him in the place of honor.

Governor Maurizio Rava was not present at the Duke's death, but he reported that the day before, when the Duke was already very weak and unable to speak, he had turned his eyes to a portrait on his dresser and then back to Rava. The governor had interpreted the Duke's mute request and the next day sent a telegram to Katherine Elkins, informing her of his death.

In his newspaper report, Rava did not mention Faduma Ali, but then neither did he refer to Katherine Elkins by name, but only as "that person." If he feared to offend the Savoys by mentioning Katherine, he certainly would not have included a statement that an African woman, member of a conquered people, was the common-law wife of a crown prince. Nevertheless, it is comforting to think that the Duke enjoyed a quiet love in the last years of his life.

Luigi di Savoia died on March 18, 1933. No one from his family was at his deathbed, and no one from his family came to his funeral. The only relative who would certainly have rushed to be near him was his sister-in-law Hélène, who was then crossing the Sahara on the back of a camel. She received the news of the Duke's death by ciphered telegram at Sebha, in Libya, and replied by wire to her family in Italy: "I received the message. Luigino is resting in peace."

The Duke was buried in the Village, in a simple tomb. King Vittorio Emanuele III visited it once in the course of a trip to Somalia in 1934 and found that it had become a place of worship for the local population, who adorned it with pillars and various objects to honor and venerate in their own way the man they considered a holy benefactor. When Hélène visited the tomb, also in 1934, she had most of the incongruous additions removed.

After the Duke's death, the Village continued to prosper, so much so that in 1992, after years of revolution, war, famine, and devastation, the major part of the country's production of sugar and oil still came from what remained of the Duke's fields and factories.

There have been great changes since 1933. When Somaliland became the independent country of Somalia in 1960, the S.A.I.S. was transformed into the S.N.A.I.—the Società Nazionale Agricola Industriale, or National Industrial Agricultural Company. Ownership of the society was divided so that 50 percent was held by the S.A.I.S. and 50 percent by the Somalian state. The Duke's house, the church, and the cemetery were put under the protection of Italy's Military Order of the Knights of Malta, who eventually replaced the aging headstone with one bearing the simple inscription "Luigi di Savoia."

Even with the change in administration, the company ran much the same. One difference was that it tended to focus on the production of sugar, which was more profitable than the other crops—despite the fact that in the past the diversification of crops had been the prime reason for its success.

After Siad Barre seized power in 1969, all foreign businesses in Somalia were nationalized, along with the 50 percent of the S.N.A.I. that belonged to the S.A.I.S. The Village continued to function and the land to produce until 1993, despite the devastations provoked by the civil war, which began in the north in 1991 and spread throughout the country. In 1993, opposing factions clashed near the Village. In Mogadishu and other cities, tombs were opened and the coffins uncovered by starving or drunken people in search of rings or any object exchangeable for food or other goods. The Knights of Malta, fearing that the Duke's tomb might be similarly desecrated, asked permission from the Somali authorities to remove his body. They had made a similar request in 1976 because of political unrest in the country, but it had been denied. A poignant explanation was given in a letter written to the Order of the Knights of Malta by the Ministry of Foreign Affairs of the Democratic Republic of Somalia:

> The People and the Government of Somalia consider the tomb of the Duke of the Abruzzi a historical monument to the memory of the person who, by his own efforts, realized the construction of the first industrial factory in Somalia setting the basis for the economic development of the Country. Therefore the Somalian Government, interpreting the feeling of the Somali People, wishes to keep the tomb of the Duke in its present place, undertaking to protect it so that the population can visit the tomb to express their feelings of memory, inasmuch as the Duke of the Abruzzi is part of the personages who have a good name in the history of Somalia.

This time, however, permission to remove the Duke's body was granted. Luigi di Savoia's grandnephew, Amedeo of Savoia-Aosta, accompanied by a contingent of the Italian army sent to Somalia to protect the return of Italian citizens, traveled to the Village to retrieve the Duke's body and found the Village destroyed—the houses unroofed, the fields devastated, and the marks of bullets on the cemetery walls. After a brief mass celebrated before the tomb, Amedeo was approached by the chief of the Village, an old man who spoke Italian and who pleaded with him not to remove the Duke's body, explaining, "This is a sacred place: we have buried our dead next to him because he protects them, and he will protect them as long as he stays here. Do not take him away!"

Amedeo was moved by this appeal. As he later related: "At the end I said to myself that my uncle Luigino had been an explorer and knew Africa well. When he decided to go to die and be buried in this country, he knew that there might be war and revolts and that his tomb might be violated; nevertheless he wanted to be buried there. I thought it my duty to respect his wish."

Thus the Duke of the Abruzzi was left in the land in which he had desired to rest in peace: a land of conquest for his Italian compatriots; for the Duke of the Abruzzi, his chosen home.

Notes

1. Aosta is a province in the Piedmont, an area in northern Italy. The Abruzzi region is located in central Italy along the coast of the Adriatic Sea.
2. Emile Rey was one of the greatest and most famous Alpine guides of the late nineteenth century. The Duke had a special affection for Rey and was devastated when he died in a fall from the Dent du Géant in 1895.
3. Modern-day climbers will recognize the Regina Margherita as a well known refuge at the summit.
4. Mummery, who had himself frequently climbed with the great guide Alexander Burgener, even expressed the opinion that it would be better to climb without guides.
5. Mummery's small expedition, which included Norman Collie, Geoffrey Hastings, Lieutenant Charles Bruce (who would later lead the 1924 British expedition to Everest), and two Gurkha porters, first attempted the Rupal Face but was defeated there by deep snow. After the climbers crossed to the Diamir Face, Collie began to suffer intestinal problems and both Hastings and Bruce started to feel the effects of altitude. Mummery and one of the porters forged ahead, reaching an altitude of nearly 21,000 feet (6,402 meters). Collie, Hastings, and Bruce then set out to reconnoiter the Rakhiot Flank of the massif, leaving Mummery and the two porters to ferry loads up from the bottom of the Rakhiot Valley to the new position. In his last letters to his wife, Mummery admitted that the scale of the mountain might be beyond his capabilities. On the morning of August 24, he and the two porters left camp and were never seen again.
6. This tale, which is repeated in all biographies of the Duke, is of questionable veracity. In the October 1898 issue of the *Revista Mensile del C.A.I.*, the Duke himself wrote about this ascent and he made no mention of Petigax's action.

7. In the English version of the book about the Mount St. Elias expedition, Sella includes a lengthy report on the types of equipment he took with him. His list includes one camera obscura (30 x 40 cm), four double frames for negatives, one rapid rectilinear Dallmeyer lens, sixty plates, one Kodak camera (13 x 18 cm), twelve double negative frames, one telephoto attachment, one double anastigmatic Ross-Goertz camera, 18 x 24 cm plates, 18 x 25 cm film, a tripod, fifteen dozen rolls of medium isochromatic films (Edwards and Co.), thirty dozen extra rolls of film. The Duke and Gonella each took a small camera as well. Sella took some of his best photos with the Kodak camera.

8. It was from the *San Martino* that Guglielmo Marconi, just a few weeks earlier, had sent his first telegraph message, contacting another wireless unit some 10 miles (16 kilometers) away and thus beginning a new era in communications.

9. Another way through the labyrinth of the Arctic had actually been found by Robert McClure in 1853.

10. Nansen's theory of polar drift was based on the fact that wreckage from a ship named the *Jeannette*, which had foundered in the ice north of the Bering Strait, had ultimately been found on the southwest coast of Greenland, apparently having been carried there by the ice.

11. Livingstone was eventually found by Henry Morton Stanley, then a fresh young journalist, on the eastern shore of Lake Tanganyika—a meeting immortalized by Stanley's understated greeting: "Doctor Livingstone, I presume."

12. Because the heights of the various Ruwenzori peaks are the subject of some discussion, the heights given in the Duke's account of the expedition are used throughout this chapter.

13. Although at this time it was still part of the Ottoman Empire, Albania was struggling for its independence and hoped to establish its own monarchy.

14. During their expedition to Nun Kun in the eastern Punjab in 1906, Fannie Bullock Workman reached the impressive altitude of 23,300 feet (7,102 meters).

15. Crowley became notorious in Victorian England. Attempting to reproduce the mystical insights he felt while climbing at altitude, he undertook a wide range of occult sexual and mental experiments, which he

then published. Known as "The Beast" and as "the wickedest man in England," Crowley was rediscovered in the permissive 1960s, when many of his works were reissued.

16. This was the site of Eckenstein's Camp X, where the expedition had stayed for a month preparing to climb the northeast spur.

17. In 1867, Austria formed a dual monarchy with Hungary, creating the Austro-Hungarian Empire, which in 1908 also annexed the provinces of Bosnia and Herzegovina. For ease of expression, this empire is referred to throughout this text simply as Austria.

18. The term "dreadnought" refers in general to a class of large, heavily armored, high-speed battleships. As a class they take their name from the *Dreadnought*, the first ship of this type, launched by the British in 1906, which weighed 20,000 tons, had a cruising speed of 21 knots, and was outfitted with ten 12-inch guns. The *Dante Aligheri* was not considered a true dreadnought, having sacrificed speed in favor of even heavier armor than usual.

19. Italy's largest source of income at this time was the some $300 million that emigrants to America and other countries annually sent back to their relatives in the homeland.

20. The Duke was particularly interested in an experimental government farm set up by Romolo Onor at Genale, near Merca. The farm failed in the end because of myriad problems, more bureacratic than operative, and Onor committed suicide in 1918. The Duke did not know him personally but held his work in high esteem and studied it in detail to avoid similar problems in setting up his own farming enterprise.

Bibliography

On the Duke of the Abruzzi

AA.VV. *Guida dell'Africa Orientale Italiana*. Milan, 1938.

AA. VV. *Dal Polo al K2 sulle orme del Duca degli Abruzzi*. Turin, 1984.

Abruzzi (Luigi Amedeo di Savoia-Aosta, Duke of the Abruzzi), U. Cagni, and A. Cavalli Molinelli, *La "Stella Polare" nel Mare Artico, 1899–1900*. Milan, 1903.

———. *Expédition de l'Etoile Polaire dans la Mer Arctique, 1899-1900*. Trans. H. Prior. Paris, 1904.

———. *On the Polar Star in the Arctic*. Trans. W. Le Queux. 2 vols. London, 1903.

———. *Il Ruwenzori, parte scientifica; Risultati delle osservazioni e studi della spedizione*, Milan, 1909.

———. *La esplorazione dello Uabi-Uebi Scebeli dalle sue sorgenti nella Etiopia Meridionale alla Somalia Italiana (1928-1929)*. Milan, 1932.

Cagni, U. *Osservazioni scientifiche eseguite durante la spedizione polare di S.A.R. Luigi Amedeo di Savoia Duca degli Abruzzi*. Milan, 1903.

Curi, E. *Il Principe Esploratore: S.A.R. il Duca degli Abruzzi*. Rovereto, 1935.

Dainelli, G. *Il Duca degli Abruzzi, Le imprese dell'ultimo grande esploratore italiano*. Turin, 1967.

De Filippi, F. *La spedizione di S.A.R. il Principe Luigi Amedeo di Savoia al Monte Sant'Elia - 1897*. Milan, 1900.

———. *The Ascent of Mount St. Elias by H.R.H. Prince Luigi Amedeo di Savoia, Duke of the Abruzzi*. Trans. L. Villari. London, 1900.

———. *Ruwenzori: An Account of the Expedition of H.R.H. Prince Luigi Amedeo di Savoia, Duke of the Abruzzi*. London, 1908.

———. *La spedizione nel Karakorum e nell'Himalaya Occidentale*. Bologna, 1911.

———. *Karakoram and the Western Himalaya 1909: Account of the Expedition of H.R.H. Prince Luigi Amedeo di Savoia*. New York, 1912.

De Filippi, F. and Luigi Amedeo di Savoia, Duke of the Abruzzi. *Il Ruwenzori*. Milan, 1908.

Degli Uberti, U. *L'Ammiraglio Luigi di Savoia Duca degli Abruzzi*. Turin, 1935.

Fabietti, E. *Vita Eroica del Duca degli Abruzzi*. Sesto S.Giovanni, 1937.

Faustini, A. *Luigi Amedeo di Savoia Duca degli Abruzzi*. Rome, n.d.

———. *Il ritorno della spedizione polare di S.A.R. il Duca degli Abruzzi*. Rome, 1900.

Jansen, P. G. *Un pioniere di Casa Savoia, S.A.R. il Duca degli Abruzzi*. Milan, 1936 (children's book).

Maino, C. *La Somalia e l'opera del Duca degli Abruzzi*. Rome, 1935.

Mangini, A. *L'opera della Società Agricola Italo-Somala in Somalia*. Milan, 1970.

Mantegazza, V. *Agli Stati Uniti. Il pericolo americano*. Milan, 1910 (about the Duke's engagement to Miss Elkins).

Michieli, A. A. *Il Duca degli Abruzzi e le sue imprese*. Milan, 1937.

Scassellati Sforzolini, G. *La Società Agricola Italo-Somala in Somalia*. Florence, 1926.

Sillani ,T. *Luigi di Savoia ammiraglio, esploratore, colono*. Rome, 1929.

Speroni, G. *Il Duca degli Abruzzi*. Milan, 1991.

On Mountaineering and Exploration

AA.VV. *La Montagna* (encyclopedia). Novara, 1984–88.

Berton, P. *The Arctic Grail: The Quest for the Northwest Passage and the North Pole, 1818–1909*. Toronto, 1988.

Bottego, V. *Il Giuba inesplorato*. 1895.

Clark, R. W. *The Splendid Hills: The Life and Photographs of Vittorio Sella 1859–1943*. London, 1948 (biography of Vittorio Sella)

Cleare, J. *The World Guide to Mountains and Mountaineering*. Exeter, England, 1979.

Collie, J. N. *The Snows of Yesteryear*. Toronto, 1973.

Desio, A. *La conquista del K2*. Milan, 1954.

Engel, C. E. *Storia dell'Alpinismo: Cento anni di alpinismo italiano* (with appendices by M. Mila). Turin, 1965.

Gessi, R. *Sette anni nel Sudan Egiziano*. Milan, 1891.

Gobetti, P. *Le esplorazioni polari*. Milan, 1959.

Maxton-Graham, J. *Safe Return Doubtful*. New York, 1988.

Moorehead, *The Blue Nile*. London, 1962.

———. *The White Nile*. London, 1960.

Mowat, F. *The Polar Passion: The Quest for the North Pole*. Vol. 2 of *Ordeal by Ice*. Toronto, 1967.

Mummery, A. F. *Le mie scalate nelle Alpi e nel Caucaso*. Turin, 1930.

———. *My Climbs in the Alps and Caucasus*. London and New York, 1895.

Parkenham, T. *The Scramble for Africa: The White Man's Conquest of the Dark Continent from 1876 to 1912*. New York, 1991.

Roberts, D. *Great Exploration Hoaxes*. San Francisco, 1982.

Rowell, G. *In the Throne Room of the Mountain Gods*. San Francisco, 1977.

Roper, S. and A. Steck. *Fifty Classic Climbs of North America*. San Francisco, 1979.

Samatar, *The State and Rural Transformation in Northern Somalia 1884–1986*. Madison, Wisc., 1989.

Scassellati, G. Sforzolini, *La Società Agricola Italo-Somala in Somalia*. Florence, 1926.

Stanley, H. M. *How I Found Livingstone*. Montreal, 1872.

Stefanini, G. and A. Desio. *Le colonie*. Turin, 1928.

Stegner, W. *North to the Pole*. New York, 1987.

Symonds, J. and K. Grant, eds. *The Confession of Aleister Crowley*. New York, 1969.

Unsworth, W. *Hold the Heights*. London, 1993.

Wilson, C. *Aleister Crowley, Nature of the Beast*. Wellingborough, Northhamptonshire, 1987.

On the History of Italy and the Savoy Family

Bartoli, D. *I Savoia, ultimo atto*. Novara, 1986.

Bertoldi, S. *Aosta, gli altri Savoia*. Milan, 1987.

Bosworth, R. J. *Italy, the Least of the Great Powers: Italian Foreign Policy before the First World War*. Cambridge, England, 1979.

———. *Italy and the Approach of the First World War*. London, 1983.

Capone, A. *Destra e Sinistra: da Cavour a Crispi*. Vol. 20 of *Storia d'Italia*. Ed. G. Galasso. Turin, 1981.

Candeloro, G. *Storia dell'Italia Moderna*, Milan, 1968.

Carocci, G. *Storia d'Italia dall'Unità ad oggi*. Milan, 1975.

Clark, M. *Longman History of Modern Italy, 1871–1982*. Vol. 7. London, 1984.

Cognasso, F. *I Savoia nella politica Europea*. Milan, 1941.

Croce, B. *La Storia d'Italia dal 1871 al 1915*. Bari, 1928.

Cunsolo, R. S. *Italian Nationalism from Its Origins to World War II*. Malabarr, Fla., 1990.

Cutolo, A. *Gli ultimi Savoia*. Salerno, 1985.

De Blasi, J. *I Savoia dalle origini al 1900*. Florence, 1940.

Gaeta, F. *La crisi di fine secolo e l'Età Giolittiana*. Vol. 21 of *Storia d'Italia*. Ed. G. Galasso. Turin, 1981.

Gunn, P. *A Concise History of Italy*. London, 1971.

Hayward, F. *Storia della Casa Savoia*. Bologna, 1955.

Katz, R. *The Fall of the House of Savoy*. London, 1972.

Mack Smith, D. *I Savoia re d'Italia*. Milan, 1990.

Mack Smith, D. *Storia d'Italia dal 1861 al 1969*. Bari, 1969.

Maria José, Queen Consort of Umberto II, King of Italy. *La Maison de Savoie*. Paris, 1956–62.

Speroni, G. *Amedeo d'Aosta, Re di Spagna*. Milan, 1985.

Villa Santa, N. and A. Valori. *Amedeo Duca d'Aosta*. Rome, 1953.

On World War I and Naval History

Chatterton, E. K. *Seas of Adventure: The Story of Naval Operations in the Mediterranean, Adriatic and Aegean*. London, 1936.

Fitzsimmons, B., ed. *Warships and Sea Battles of World War I*. London, 1936.

Halpern, P. G. *A Naval History of World War I*. Annapolis, 1994.

Hough, R. *The Great War at Sea, 1914–1918*. New York, 1983.

Joll, J. *Origins of the First World War*. London, 1984.

Kerr, Admiral M. *Land, Sea and Air*. London, 1927.

Marder, A. J. *Portrait of an Admiral: The Life and Papers of Sir Herbert Richmond*. London, 1952.

Whittam, J. and G. Helm. *The Politics of the Italian Army*. Hamden, Conn., 1977.

Magazines, Newspapers, Special Issues
British and American Magazines

Alpine Journal (Alpine Club, London, unless otherwise noted):

"Ascents in the Alps by the Duke of the Abruzzi." No. 16, pp. 272, and No. 18, pp. 286, 409, 521.

"The Expedition of H.R.H. Prince Louis of Savoy, Duke of the Abruzzi, to Mount St. Elias, Alaska." No. 19 (1898), pp. 116–128. (Royal Geographical Society, London)

"Ascent of Punta Jolanda, Dames Anglaises." No. 21, p. 11.

"Expedition to Ruwenzori." No. 23, pp. 173, 242, 310, 386.

"Expedition to Himalaya." No. 24, p. 688.

"The Expedition of H.R.H. the Duke of the Abruzzi to the Karakoram Himalayas." No. 25 (1910), pp. 107–111 (Royal Geographical Society, London), and pp. 331, 479. (Alpine Club, London)

"War Service." No. 29, p. 275.

"Luigi Amedeo di Savoia, Duke of the Abruzzi (obituary by Filippo De Filippi)." No. 45, pp. 201–215.

American Alpine Club Journal: Obituary. No. 247 (November 1933).

Autocar Report: Vol. 7, no. 318 (November 30, 1901.)

Bystander (Alpine Club of London): January 23, 1907.

Geographical Journal:

"The Italian Arctic Expedition 1899–1900." No. 18 (1901), pp. 282–294.

"L. A.di Savoia, The Snows of the Nile, being an account of the exploration of the peaks, passes and glaciers of Ruwenzori." No. 24 (February 1907).

"The Expedition of H.R.H. the Duke of the Abruzzi to the Karakoram Himalayas." No. 25 (1910), pp. 107–111. (Royal Geographical Society, London)

"The Expedition of the Duke of the Abruzzi to the Karakoram Himalayas." (January 1911), pp. 19–30.

Ingraham, E. S. "The Ascent of Mount St. Elias." *The Mountaineer Annual* 27, 1 (Dec. 15, 1924).

Lara, R. and F. Reichel. "The Adventures of a Modern Prince." *McClure's Magazine* 34, 6 (April 1910).

Nature: "Recensione del libro di De Filippi sul St.Elia." Vol. 62, no. 1592 (May 3, 1900). (Alpine Club, London)

Tour du Monde: "L'Etoile Polaire dans la mer Arctique (1899–1900) par S.A.S. le Duc des Abruzzes. Translated and summarized by H. Prior." No. 9 (1903), pp. 145–228 (Royal Geographical Society, London)

Whymper, E. "The Exploits of the Duke of the Abruzzi." *The Wide World Magazine* (1909).

Italian Magazines

Associazione dell'Arma di Cavalleria: "La morte di S.A.R. il duca degli Abruzzi (obituary)." No. 4 (April 1933).

Bragadin, M. "Il Principe delle solitudini." *Oggi* (1949), nos. 47–52. (Archivio Rizzoli)

Bollettino della Società Geografica Italiana (Royal Geographical Society, London, unless otherwise noted):

"Spedizione Italiana nel Mare Artico sulla 'Stella Polare.' Conferenza di S.A.R. il Duca degli Abruzzi e del Comandante U. Cagni." No. 2 (1901), pp. 121–180.

"La Conferenza del Duca degli Abruzzi e del Comandante Cagni alla Società Geografica Italiana." No. 8 (1901), pp. 49–59.

"La spedizione di S.A.R. il Duca degli Abruzzi al Ruwenzori." No. 8 (1907), pp. 99–127.

"La spedizione di S.A.R. il Duca degli Abruzzi all'Himalaya e Karakorum." Fasc. 4, 11 (1910), pp. 435–469.

"Esplorazione dei monti del Karakorum." Fasc. 4 (1910). (Alpine Club, London)

"La spedizione di S.A.R. il Duca degli Abruzzi alle sorgenti dell'Webi-Shebelle." Fasc. 6, 6 (1929), pp. 359–371.

Bosazza, F. "Il Duca degli Abruzzi al Monte St. Elia nell'Alasca." *La Rassegna Nazionale* (April 1898) (estratto) (Alpine Club, London)

Le Comunicazioni di un Collega: "Esplorazioni verso i Poli. La spedizione del duca degli Abruzzi." Vol. 8, nos. 1, 2 (1901).

Cosmos: "La spedizone di S.A.R. il Duca degli Abruzzi al Polo Nord. Umberto Cagni raggiunge 86°33'49"." No. 13 (1901), pp. 30–40. Cenni Generali di Guido Cora (Royal Geographical Society, London)

De Meis, D. M. "Luigi di Savoia Duca degli Abruzzi (obituary)." *L'Enciclopedico* (Rome 1933). (Archivio di Stato di Turin,, Duca d'Aosta, CS 6 n° 82)

Elena di Francia, Duchessa d'Aosta. "Giornale di viaggio." *Nuova Antologia* (1935). (Archivio di Stato di Turin, Duca d'Aosta, CS 6 n° 82)

Emporium:

Vol. 11, pp. 163-165; vol. 12, p. 255; vol. 18, p. 240; vol. 20, p. 158.

"Spedizione del Duca degli Abruzzi al Polo Nord." Vol. 13, p. 82.

"Viaggio al Ruwenzori." Vol. 25, p. 386.

"Spedizione al Karakorum." Vol. 30, p. 361.

"Spedizione al Karakorum." *L'Esplorazione Commerciale*. No. 25 (1910), pp. 33–43 (Royal Geographical Society, London)

Milanese, E. "Storia di una bonifica coloniale: la nascita della Società Agricola Italo-Somala (S.A.I.S.)." *Rivista di Storia dell'Agricoltura* 35, 2 (December 1995).

―――. "Tra Sardegna e Somalia: storia di due bonifiche nella corrispondenza fra il Duca degli Abruzzi e Vittorio Sella." *I Georgofili*. Atti dell'Accademia XLII, serie settima (Conference held at the Accademia dei Georgofili, June 8, 1995).

Piccioli. "Il grande pioniere della Somalia, Luigi Amedeo di Savoia, Duca degli Abruzzi (obituary)." *L'Impero Coloniale Fascista* (1936), p. 377.

Rivista del Club Alpino Italiano:

"Ascensioni sulle Alpi" (1892), nn. 248, 277.

"Ascensioni sulle Alpi" (1894), nn. 219, 245.

"Luigi de Savoia Aosta, Duca degli Abruzzi, Presidente onorario sez. Turin, e pergamena" (1894), nn. 294, 305.

"Socio onorario Club Alpino Francese" (1895), n. 186.

"Ascensione invernale al Monviso" (1897), n. 73.

"Socio onorario Sezione Milan" (1897), nr. 457.

"Spedizione al St.Elia" (1897), nn. 167, 232, 281, 359, 409 (relazione spedizione), 443.

"Due nuove ascensioni nel gruppo del Monte Bianco (Aiguille Sans Nom e Punta Margherita)" (1898), nn. 292, 417.

"Elargizione al C.A.I." (1897), n. 465.

"Spedizione al St.Elia" (1899), n. 437.

"Spedizione polare" (1899), n. 191.

"Spedizione polare" (1900), n. 309 (Ritorno); n. 443 (Onoranze).

"Spedizione polare"(1901), nn. 19, 52 (Conferenze).

"Onoranze ai compagni" (1900), n. 20.

"Elargizione a favore cassa soccorso guide" (1900), n. 156.

"Prima ascensione della Punta Jolanda alle Dames Anglaises (1900), nn. 277, 365.

"Spedizione Polare" (1902), n. 193 (medaglia d'onore).

"Dono al C.A.I. di strumenti" (1902), n. 257.

"Dono al C.A.I. dei volumi sulla spedizione" (1902), n. 453.

"Osservazioni scientifiche eseguite durante la spedizione polare" (1903), n. 146.

"Socio onorario della S.A.T."(1906), n. 340.

"Spedizione al Ruwenzori" (1906), nn. 196, 237.

"Conferenze a Roma e a Londra" (1907), nn. 1, 10.

"Premio per le Guide" (1906), n. 124.

"Relazione di De Filippi sulla spedizione al Ruwenzori" (1909), n. 21.

"Spedizione polare" (1909), n. 174.

"Spedizione al Karakorum" (1909), nn. 113, 281.

"Record di altitudine raggiunto" (1910), n. 36.

"Cassa pensione per la Guide del Consorzio Alpi Occidentali" (1911), n. 162.

"Spedizione al Karakorum" (1912), n. 163.

"Viaggio di esplorazione in Somalia" (1919), n. 179.

"Socio onorario del C.A.I." (1923), nn. 49, 95.

"Discoso all'inaugurazione del monumento a G. Petigax" (1928), n. 223.

"Accademico Alpinista" (1930), n. 740.

"Medaglia d'oro" (1930), nn. 178, 179.

"Necrologi e commemorazioni" (1933), nn. 175, 231 (Manaresi), 234 (De Filippi), 444, 620. (P.Guiton) "Lapide al Giomein" (1933), n. 563.

"Commemorazioni" (1934), n. 51 (a Praga), n. 107.

"Crociera commemorativa in Somalia" (1934), n. 216.

"Principe Esploratore" (1935), n. 331.

"Progetto monumento a Courmayeur" (1936), n. XVII.

"Commemorazione" (1937), n. XXVII.

"Le Imprese del Duca degli Abruzzi" (1938), nn. 180, 331.

"Le spedizioni extraeuropee del Duca degli Abruzzi (al Museo Nazionale della Montagna)" (1942), n. 219.

"Lapide al campo base della spedizione italiana al K2" (1954), n. 407.

"Lettera di invito a Vittorio Sella per partecipare alla spedizione del K2 (v. anche documenti originali Fondazione Sella)" (1954), n. 408.

Saini, E. "Il Principe delle leggendarie esplorazioni." *Settimo Giorno*, no. 20 (1963). (Archivio Rizzoli)

Lo Scarpone: "Il Nostro Duca. Il lutto delle guide valdostane." (April 1, 1933). (Fondazione Sella)

Untitled article about S.A.I.S. *L'Italia Coloniale* 11 (1934).

British and American Newspapers

American Weekly: "Why Billy Hitt Wasn't a 'Hit' as a Husband." 1923 (Archivio di Stato di Turin, Duca d'Aosta, CS 6 n° 82)

Eastern Daily: "Duke of the Abruzzi on the Snows of the Nile." January 14, 1907(Fondazione Sella)

London Daily Telegraph:
"Duke's Ruwenzori Speech." January 1907.
"The Duke of the Abruzzi—A Great Explorer (obituary)." March 25, 1933.

London Times: January 1873.

Manchester Guardian:
"A Royal Mountain Explorer, by Sir Martin Conway (review of De Filippi's book on Mt. St. Elias)." February 3, 1900.
"Queen Peaks of Africa. Italian Prince's Feat." January 1, 1907.

Newcastle Leader: "The Ascent of Mount St. Elias." September 11, 1897.

New York Post: "The Duke of the Abruzzi's Recent Expedition." January 8, 1907.

New York Times:
"Duke of the Abruzzi Conquers the Mountains of the Moon." October 7, 1906.
"The Duke of the Abruzzi and Mount Ruwenzori." January 8, 1907.
"Duke meets Peary." May 28, 1907.

Pall Mall Gazette: January 14, 1907.

Victoria Daily Colonist: May 17, 1897 and August 26, 1897.

Italian Newspapers

Corriere della Sera:
"Il 'match' automobilistico fra il Duca degli Abruzzi e il cav. Coltelletti." November 25–26, 1901, p. 3.
"Ancora sul match automobilistico." November 26–27, 1901, p. 2.
"Lo sbarco a Napoli del Duca degli Abruzzi reduce dal viaggio alle sorgenti dello Scebeli (dateline Naples, signed L. B.)." April 19, 1929, p. 3.
"Il Duca degli Abruzzi parla all'Augusteo sul recente viaggio di esplorazione in Etiopia (dateline Rome, May 17, unsigned)." May 18, 1929, p. 5.

Obituary (cable from Mussolini). March 20, 1933.

Gazzetta del Popolo della Sera: "La prima narrazione degli ultimi giorni di Luigi di Savoia. Come morì il Duca degli Abruzzi." March 21–22, 1938.

Giornale d'Italia: "Rientro del DdA di ritorno da un'esplorazione in Somalia (signed L. Lo Sardo) (obituary and cables from Mussolini and Federzoni). July 25, 1920 (21.3. anno XI), p. 3.

Nuovo Giornale: Obituary. March 20, 1933.

Il Piccolo. Obituary (cable from Mussolini). March 20,1933, p. 3.

Unidentified clipping dated February 18. "Perché Don Ratti non andò al Polo." (Fondazione Sella)

Leaflets and Booklets (AST=Archivio di Stato di Turin, Duca d'Aosta, CS 6, n°82).

Amante, A. "Luigi Savoia Duca degli Abruzzi." Turin, 1950. (AST)

Brocherel, G. "La scalata dell'Himalaya: La Spedizione del Duca degli Abruzzi." (AST)

Bruno, L. "In memoria del Duca degli Abruzzi." Atti dell'VII Convegno Italo-Africano. Milan, 1959.

De Filippi, F. "Commemorazione." Turin, 1933. (AST)

Gonella, F. "Ascensioni del Duca degli Abruzzi - 1884. Estratto CAI. Turin, 1985. (AST)

Pagano di Melito, G. "Il Principe Marinaro." Rome, 1934 (AST)

Ponti, A. "Luigi di Savoia Italiano Nuovo." Rome, 1934 (AST)

Ricci, L. "Commemorazione di S.A.R. il Duca degli Abruzzi." Venice, 1933. (AST)

Vallauri, G. "Commemorazione." Rome, 1933. (AST))

Vecchi, B. V. "LS DdA Pioniere Africano." Milan, 1973. (AST)

Appendices

I.

Comparative Chronology

Date	The World	Italy	Duke of the Abruzzi
1873	H. M. Stanley leaves Africa; Livingstone dies.		Born in Madrid, Spain, January 29; his father, Prince Amedeo, abdicates Spanish throne.
1876	Bell invents telephone; Custer's Last Stand	Explorer Romolo Gessi first sees Ruwenzori mountains.	Death of his mother when he is three and a half.
1878		Death of Vittorio Emanuele II; Umberto I ascends throne of Italy.	
1879	Edison patents light bulb; Mummery's first ascent of Matterhorn's Zmutt Ridge.		Enters military school at age six.
1889	Eiffel Tower completed; Menelik II becomes Emperor of Ethiopia.		Promoted to midshipman at sixteen; first world voyage on *Amerigo Vespucci*.

Year			
1890			Upon his father's death, becomes Duke of the Abruzzi at age seventeen; promoted to 2nd Lt.; meets Umberto Cagni on the *Vespucci*.
1892	Conway attempts Chogolisa in the Karakoram		Climbs Punta Levanna, western Alps.
1893	Norwegian Fridtjof Nansen sets out *Fram*	Italy annexes Somaliland; peasant troubles in Italy; Margherita climbs Punta Gnifetti.	Sails to Somaliland on board the *Volturno*
1894			Climbs Zmutt Ridge on Matterhorn with Mummery and Collie; admitted to Alpine Club in London.
1895	Mummery killed on Nanga Parbat; Duke's guide Guido Rey killed climbing the Dent du Géant.	Tafari Maconnén defeats Italian troops at Amba Alagi.	World circumnavigation on board the *Cristoforo Columbo*.
1896	Nansen reaches farthest north latitude to date.	Italian army annihilated at Adawa, Ethiopia; bread riots across Italy.	Hires Joseph Petigax as guide; returns from voyage vowing to climb Nanga Parbat.
1897	Klondike Gold Rush in Alaska.	Duke's yacht *Bona* revolutionizes international yacht racing.	Leads his first expedition, to Mt. St. Elias.
1898	Account of Mt. St. Elias expedition published.	*Bona* completes second successful season.	With Cagni travels to Spitzbergen Islands to research Arctic waters.
1899			Leads North Pole expedition on *Polar Star*.

Year			
1900	Puccini debuts *Madame Butterfly* and *La Tosca.*	King Umberto assassinated July 29; son Vittorio Emanuele III becomes king.	Cagni establishes new farthest north mark.
1901	Mombasa railway completed to Lake Victoria.	Composer Verdi dies; large-scale strikes across Italy.	Duke races Coltelletti in auto race; climbs Dames Anglaises; promoted to captain of *Liguria.*
1903			Receives medal from American explorer Robert Peary in New York; promotes Pole book; departs on another world cruise.
1905	Japan defeats Russia in sea battle.		Begins planning African expedition.
1906	San Francisco earthquake and fire; first British dreadnought launched;	Vesuvius erupts.	Leads Ruwenzori expedition in Africa.
1907	Peary claims to have beaten Italian farthest north record.		Gives lecture in London attended by King Edward VII; sails to America, meets Katherine Elkins.
1908	Peary departs for North Pole.	Earthquake and tidal wave in Sicily kill 150,000 people.	Returns to America incognito to meet Miss Elkins.
1909	Peary claims to have reached the North Pole.	First Italian dreadnought launched.	K2 expedition departs in secret; Italians claim new altitude record.
1911	Senator Elkins, Katherine's father, dies; Norwegian Roald Amundsen reaches South Pole, December 16.		Leads first naval battle in Libyan War.

Year			
1912	*Titanic* sinks, 1,513 drowned; British party under Robert F. Scott perishes on return from South Pole.	Italy renews Triple Alliance with Germany and Austria.	Assigned command of the dreadnought *Regina Elena*.
1913	Kaiser Wilhelm II hosts Duke and King Vittorio Emanuele III at Kielerwoche yacht races.		Releases Katherine Elkins from their engagement; she marries Billy Hitt; despite speculation, the Duke is not named king of Albania.
1914	Archduke Ferdinand of Austria assassinated in Sarajevo.	Italy remains neutral.	Promoted to admiral.
1915		Italy joins England, France, and Russia in war against Germany and Austria.	Given supreme command of joint naval forces in the Adriatic.
1916		War goes badly for Italian military forces.	Leads rescue of 160,000 Serbian soldiers.
1917			Relieved of his command, leaves naval service.
1918	First World War ends.		Makes first exploratory trip to Somaliland.
1919		Mussolini forms Fasci Italiani di Combattimento.	Selects site for his experimental colony.
1920	Peary dies.		

Year			
1921	First British expedition to Mt. Everest from Tibet.		Raises funds for Duke of the Abruzzi Village.
1922	Duke's altitude record broken by second British expediton to Everest.	King Vittorio Emanuele III turns government over to Mussolini.	Construction of Village begins at Giohàr.
1924	Mallory and Irvine disappear near summit of Mt. Everest.		Named Senator of the Realm under Mussolini.
1926	Duke of Spoleto, nephew of the Duke of Abruzzi, leads expedition to Baltoro and K2.	Death of Queen Mother Margherita.	Death of Joseph Petigax.
1928		As Ambassador to Ethiopia, the Duke leads negotiations for friendship treaty.	Organizes Webi-Shebelle expedition to the river's source in Ethiopia.
1929	Worldwide financial failures; beginning of Great Depression.		Returns to Italy; conducts lecture series; cancer discovered.
1930	Nansen dies.		
1931			Duke's eldest brother, Emanuele Filiberto dies; death of Umberto Cagni.
1933	Fourth British expedition to Everest.		Returns to Somaliland; dies in Village at age sixty.

Family Tree

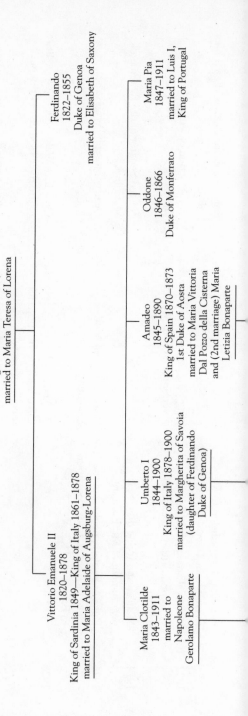

Carlo Alberto
1789–1849
King of Sardinia 1831–1849
married to Maria Teresa of Lorena

Vittorio Emanuele II
1820–1878
King of Sardinia 1849—King of Italy 1861–1878
married to Maria Adelaide of Augsburg-Lorena

Ferdinando
1822–1855
Duke of Genoa
married to Elisabeth of Saxony

Maria Clotilde
1843–1911
married to
Napoleone
Gerolamo Bonaparte

Umberto I
1844–1900
King of Italy 1878–1900
married to Margherita of Savoia
(daughter of Ferdinando
Duke of Genoa)

Amadeo
1845–1890
King of Spain 1870–1873
1st Duke of Aosta
married to Maria Vittoria
Dal Pozzo della Cisterna
and (2nd marriage) Maria
Letizia Bonaparte

Oddone
1846–1866
Duke of Monferrato

Maria Pia
1847–1911
married to Luis I,
King of Portugal

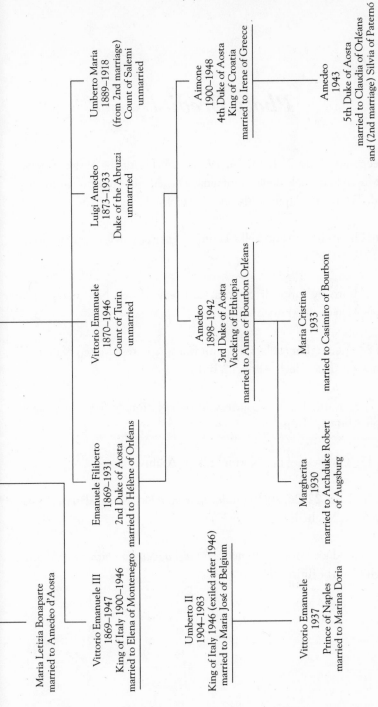

Maria Letizia Bonaparte
married to Amedeo d'Aosta

Vittorio Emanuele III
1869–1947
King of Italy 1900–1946
married to Elena of Montenegro

Emanuele Filiberto
1869–1931
2nd Duke of Aosta
married to Hélène of Orléans

Vittorio Emanuele
1870–1946
Count of Turin
unmarried

Luigi Amedeo
1873–1933
Duke of the Abruzzi
unmarried

Umberto Maria
1889–1918
(from 2nd marriage)
Count of Salemi
unmarried

Umberto II
1904–1983
King of Italy 1946 (exiled after 1946)
married to Maria José of Belgium

Amedeo
1898–1942
3rd Duke of Aosta
Viceking of Ethiopia
married to Anne of Bourbon Orléans

Aimone
1900–1948
4th Duke of Aosta
King of Croatia
married to Irene of Greece

Vittorio Emanuele
1937
Prince of Naples
married to Marina Doria

Margherita
1930
married to Archduke Robert
of Augsburg

Maria Cristina
1933
married to Casimiro of Bourbon

Amedeo
1943
5th Duke of Aosta
married to Claudia of Orléans
and (2nd marriage) Silvia of Paternó

Photo Credits

Frontispiece and plates 2, 4, 13, 14, 19, 21, 23: Photos by Vittorio Sella, courtesy Museo Nazionale della Montagna "Duca degli Abruzzi," Turin, and Instituto de Fotografia Alpina "Vittorio Sella," Biella

Plates 3, 6: Photos by Vittorio Sella, courtesy Instituto de Fotografia Alpina "Vittorio Sella," Biella

Plate 20: Photo by Luigi de Savoia, courtesy Museo Nazionale della Montagna "Duca degli Abruzzi," Turin

Plates 27, 28, 30-32: Photos by Giovanni Braca, courtesy Museo Nazionale della Montagna "Duca degli Abruzzi," Turin

Plates 1, 7, 8, 9, 10, 11, 33: Courtesy Museo Nazionale della Montagna "Duca degli Abruzzi," Turin

Plates 16, 17: Courtesy of Lee Norton, Elkins Archives

Plates 5, 12, 15, 18, 22, 26, 29: Reproduced from *Il Duca degli Abruzzi e le sue imprese* by A. A. Michieli (Milan, 1937)

Plate 25: Reproduced from *L'Ammiraglio Luigi de Savoia Duca degli Abruzzi* by U. Degli Uberti (Turin, 1935).

Index

About the Authors

MIRELLA TENDERINI is a well-known author, mountaineering journalist, and literary agent, who has climbed extensively across Europe. She writes for *Alp*, *La Revista della Montagna*, *Mountain*, *Desnivel*, and other international mountaineering journals and is the author of a biography of the American mountaineer Gary Hemming. She lives in Italy.

MICHAEL SHANDRICK has trekked and climbed in the Himalaya, Central America, and the Sierra Nevada. His outdoor writings and reviews of mountaineering books have appeared in *Outside*, *Summit*, *Climbing*, *The San Jose Mercury News*, *The Berkeley Monthly*, and *The San Francisco Chronicle*. He lives in Vancouver, British Columbia, and is currently working on a mountaineering adventure novel.